Bellevue

INVITATION TO DINE

Published by Doubleday
a division of Random House, Inc.
1540 Broadway, New York, New York 10036

Doubleday and the portrayal of an anchor with a dolphin are trademarks
of Doubleday, a division of Random House, Inc.

ISBM 0-385-4982-6

Printed in Germany
First English Edition published by Doubleday, November 2000

©   Verlag
       Zabert Sandmann, Munich

Photography	Christian von Alvensleben
Editor	Monika Kellermann
Editorial Assistant	Otto Koch
Graphic design	Zero, Munich
Production	Karin Mayer, Peter Karg-Cordes
Lithography	inteca Media Service GmbH, Rosenheim
Printing/Binding	Mohndruck, Gütersloh
Translation	Karen Green, in association with
	First Edition Translations Ltd., Cambridge, UK
Realization of the American edition	First Edition Translations Ltd., Cambridge, UK

RECIPES FROM MY PERSONAL
COLLECTION

INVITATION
TO DINE

CHRISTIANE HERZOG

DOUBLEDAY

New York London Toronto Sydney Auckland

Contents

Zucker – Bretzeln

Rühre 12 Lo... ...zu Schaum,

My recipe book

In the following pages, I hope to introduce you to the recipes
that my family, and I, enjoy most.
The majority of these recipes come from cookbooks
that both my grandmothers, my mother-in-law,
one of my great-grandmothers, and other members
of my family wrote in their own hands.
I have also taken a few recipes from old,
printed cookbooks belonging to my family,
that are classic cookbooks of their day.
I have been collecting these recipes for some time,
with the vague notion of one day compiling them into
a little cookbook for my family.
But, as so often happens,
it was just wishful thinking because,
like most people, I never seem to have enough time.
In recent years my husband's job,
and my social commitments, have taken up a lot of my time.

Thus, when Dieter Hanitzsch asked me to consider
whether I might like to share my little,
informal collection of recipes with a wider audience,
I quickly warmed to the idea.

A number of recipes include raw eggs. It is advisable not to serve those dishes to
very young children, pregnant women, elderly people or anyone weakened by
serious illness. If in any doubt, consult your doctor. Of course, be sure that
all the eggs you use are as fresh as possible.

Style of cuisine

Anyone reading the recipes in this book will quickly realize
that most of them date back many years.
In those times a housewife didn't put a roast on the table every day,
in fact probably not at all on weekdays.
She was far more likely to provide a meal based on pasta or potatoes.
Menus were much more modest than they are today.

Working conditions were different too.
There were very few labor-saving gadgets,
so housewives either had to devote the whole morning to cooking,
or at least have a maid to help lighten the load.
Certainly the prevailing conditions influenced the choice of dishes.
Then, as now, a one-pot dish accompanied by a salad took
up considerably less time than a roast, or a sweet or savory strudel.

It was interesting to discover, from the cookbooks,
and slips of paper with recipes scribbled on them,
the houses, or at least the towns, where my grandmothers
and great-grandmother learned to cook.
The trail lead mainly to Nürnberg and Regensburg and,
in one case, as far afield as Vienna.
I also discovered a Franconian connection through my mother's
family, whose ancestors contributed dishes from the Vogtland.

No-one will be surprised to learn that my cuisine is
predominantly southern German in style.
It may remind you of your homeland, or of a holiday,
but in any case the recipes are so tasty, it's worth trying them.

Initially the recipes contained many culinary terms,
and names for foods that were particular to the area where the
recipe originated, as well as old weights and measures,
such as *Seidel* and *Schoppen*, which varied according to
the part of the country. They are no longer used;
indeed, there is hardly anyone nowadays who remembers them,
and so they have been converted to modern ingredients,
weights, and measures.

Regional variations in cuisine can best be shown using red
cabbage as an example. In German it can be called either
Kraut or *Kohl*, depending purely on where you come from,
but it can also be called *blau* (blue) or *rot* (red). There is
a perfectly good reason for this: in southern Germany red
cabbage is usually cooked with red wine, or red wine vinegar,
which does make the cabbage turn purplish-blue,
whereas the white wine or white wine vinegar used in
other areas of the country means the cabbage retains its red color.

The recipe collection

On the one hand these recipes reflect my family's traditions, on the other stages in my own life. Because I grew up in the Allgäu region, there was no way I could omit *Käsespatzen* and *Quarknudeln*, which are called *Ziegernudeln* in the Allgäu. The *Maultaschen* (ravioli) are carried over from my time in Baden-Württemberg, and I was served Upper Palatinate *Dotsch*, which went by the name *Pillekuchen* during our years in Bonn. I have taken care to suggest the simplest possible recipes, which are not particularly demanding, either from the point of view of culinary expertise, or ingredients. But even in the case of this good, plain cooking, careful preparation, and top quality ingredients make an important contribution to the overall result.

Timetable for a dinner party

Throughout my life I have been ruled by my appointments diary.
When I worked as a home economics teacher,
keeping to a strict timetable was always a necessity,
whether for preparation of the lesson or the teaching itself
in the school kitchen. I still can't bear to waste time today.
I even plan a private dinner party, for example, very carefully,
so that I can manage everything effortlessly on my own.
You will see how I do it from the following menu and timetable.

My timetable for a dinner party of eight

– Small mixed salad, vinaigrette dressing –
– Marinated rump or silverside of veal with spätzle –
– Cranberries and red cabbage –
– Cinnamon parfait with plum coulis –

The cornerstone of a well-planned dinner party is careful shopping. It is better not to leave anything to chance. Meat, in particular, must be ordered in good time to be sure of getting the cut you need. In the past I always stored a wide range of different types of meat in my deep freeze because I bought meat direct from the farm. Nowadays I would order the veal rump from an organic butcher. I get the best quality lamb and poultry from my local butcher.

If this precise planning seems too detailed, or even too much like hard work, careful organization prevents unwanted mishaps. A shopping list, drawn up carefully from the recipes, may mean that you don't forget that carton of cream, or the bacon for larding the veal.

Two days before:

– Do the main shop, based on the recipes –
– Place the veal rump or silverside in the marinade –
– Macerate the plums in the red wine –

One day before
– Turn the veal rump in the marinade –
– Prepare the spätzle, cook them, refresh them in cold water and put them in
an ovenproof dish, then refrigerate them –
– Cook the red cabbage, transfer it to a dish, cover and refrigerate it –
– Prepare the cinnamon parfait and freeze it –
– Add more red wine to the plums, if necessary –

Day of the dinner party
During the afternoon, set the table, choose the wine and chill it, if necessary.

6:00 p.m.	Put the veal in the oven. Cook the plums, and purée them.
6:00 – 6:30 p.m.	Wash the salad, prepare it, and refrigerate it. Prepare the vinaigrette dressing.
6:30 – 7:00 p.m.	Baste the veal, put the cranberries into a dish, and refrigerate them. Put the spätzle in the oven, and the red cabbage on the stove.
7:00 – 7:30 p.m.	Time for the hostess to freshen up and change. Baste the veal.
7:30 p.m.	Guests arrive. Serve champagne, sparkling wine, or dessert wine as an aperitif.
7:50 p.m.	Arrange the salad on the plates, and drizzle with vinaigrette. Warm the dishes and serving plates, and baste the veal.
8:00 p.m.	Dot the spätzle with butter, and warm through at 300°F. Warm the red cabbage gently. Serve the salad with a fruity white wine. Remove the cranberries from the refrigerator.
8:20 – 8:35 p.m.	Slice the veal, and keep it warm, reduce the meat juices until thick and smooth. Arrange the veal on a warmed serving dish, and serve the gravy in a gravy boat. Transfer the spätzle, and red cabbage, to warmed dishes.
8:35 p.m.	Serve the main course with a full flavored white wine. Take the parfait out of the freezer, and put it in the refrigerator.
9:10 p.m.	Warm the plum coulis. Turn out the parfait, and slice it.
9:20 p.m.	Serve the dessert with champagne, or with the red wine used to macerate the plums (a little unusual, but appropriate here).

*A*s much as I enjoy a starter during a stylish meal in a restaurant, I seldom prepare one at home. If you have to provide a family with lunch and dinner, day in, day out, elegant starters usually fall by the wayside. This is why my book does not start with the usual chapter on hors d'œuvres and appetizers, although some of the following recipes would be very suitable. I prefer to suggest recipes for light dishes, sauces, and salads that can be served either as an hors d'œuvre, or as a snack or light supper dish.

I have gathered a colorful potpourri of recipes from which I am sure, with a little imagination, you will be able to devise delicious new dishes. You can prepare every salad with, for example, the Vinaigrette Dressing or Mayonnaise. My family like spicy sauces and thus I have invented many over the years. I'm happy to pass on the recipes for some of them to you now. Young and old alike enjoy flavorful sauces, whether served at a barbecue or as a party dip.

The kohlrabi salad on page 33 might, perhaps, be new to some of you. However easy the recipe might seem, I think it's a particularly good one. In my opinion the simplest dishes are frequently the best. Try this salad with cold roast meat, barbecued meat, or simply with bread and butter. Speaking of bread and butter – a well-seasoned whole wheat or whole grain bread, spread lavishly with rich, creamy butter is, to me, a pleasure that takes some beating. The quality says it all!

Chicken Liver Terrine
(Geflügelleberpastete)

Serves 4

For the puff pastry:
1 tablespoon butter, 1 cup all-purpose flour, Pinch of salt
8–9 tablespoons cold water, 1 cup butter, chilled and diced
For the filling:
10 ounces chicken livers, 2 tablespoons butter, 14 ounces boneless shoulder of veal
4 ounces bacon, 1¾ pounds ground veal, 2 ounces plain, unflavored breadcrumbs
2 onions, sliced, 6 small mushrooms, sliced, 3 juniper berries, crushed
½ clove of garlic, crushed, 2 eggs, beaten, 2½ tablespoons medium sherry
Salt and freshly ground pepper to taste
Paprika and freshly grated nutmeg to taste, 1 egg yolk

1. For the pastry: Rub the butter into the flour, add the salt and cold water and knead to a firm, smooth dough. Refrigerate for 15 minutes.

2. Roll out the pastry into an oblong, dot 1 cup chilled butter over the pastry, then fold one third edge over to the center and then the other third over that. The result should be three equal layers on top of each other. Give the dough a quarter turn and roll out again. Repeat the folding process again, then cover the pastry and let it rest for 10 minutes.

3. Roll out again, starting from the long side. Fold over again and leave to rest for a further 10 minutes. Repeat this process twice, then leave to rest in the refrigerator, preferably overnight. (Remember to bring it back to room temperature before use.)

4. For the filling: Trim, wash, and dice the chicken livers. Melt the butter in a skillet and sear the chicken livers in the hot butter. Grind the veal shoulder and bacon together. Combine this with the ground veal and put the whole mixture through the grinder again. Combine the breadcrumbs, onions, mushrooms, juniper

berries, garlic, beaten eggs, and sherry with the ground meats and season with salt, pepper, paprika, and grated nutmeg.

5. Preheat the oven to 350°F. Rinse out a large loaf pan with cold water. Roll out two-thirds of the pastry and use it to line the pan. Fill the pastry case with half the meat mixture, layer the chicken livers on top and finish off with the remaining meat mixture. Press down firmly. Roll out the remaining pastry and use it to cover the loaf pan.

6. Pierce some small holes in the pastry lid. Roll out any pastry trimmings, cut them into fancy shapes to decorate the pastry lid. Beat the egg yolk lightly and glaze the lid. Stand the loaf pan in a roasting pan and fill with hot water to approximately half way up the sides of the loaf pan. Put the roasting pan in the preheated oven and bake for 2 hours. Check occasionally to ensure that the water has not evaporated, and top up as necessary.

7. Leave the terrine to cool in the tin, then remove it and store it in the refrigerator for at least 2 days before serving.

Grandmother's Beef Brawn
(Fleischsülze Großmutters Verfahrensweise)

Serves 6–8

2 calf's feet, 2 pig's ears, I pig's trotter,
I pound beef (silverside or thick flank), 3 carrots, 2 parsley roots,
I–2 large onions, each studded with 4–5 cloves
I slice of lemon, a few peppercorns and 2 bay leaves, Salt
Whites of 2 eggs, About I cup vinegar

1. Rinse the calf's feet, pig's ears, pig's trotter, and beef. Wash, peel, and finely chop the carrots and parsley roots. Put the meat, carrots and parsley roots in a large saucepan or stockpot with the onions, slice of lemon, peppercorns, and bay leaves. Cover the meat and vegetables with water.

2. Bring the pan to a boil slowly over a medium heat. Skim off the foam several times as it forms. Test the meat occasionally and, just as it is starting to tenderize, season the stock with salt.

3. Remove the tender beef and other meats from the saucepan, bring the stock to a fast boil and reduce the liquid by about one third. Then take the pan off the heat and skim the fat off the stock with a tablespoon. Leave the stock and meat to cool.

4. Whisk the egg whites lightly and stir them into the stock. Line a sieve with cheesecloth, warm the stock and strain it through the sieve, reserving the liquid.

5. Chop the cooled beef into small dice or thin strips. Put the chopped beef into a terrine, loaf tin, or large glass dish.

6. Season the stock very heavily with salt and vinegar. It should taste very acidic and salty. Pour the stock over the beef until it is completely covered. Put the brawn in the refrigerator and allow it to set for at least 24 hours.

If you want to serve the brawn as an hors d'œuvre,
put the chopped beef and stock into small ramekins or cups.
To serve, turn out onto a bed of salad.

Meat Salad
(Fleischsalat)

Serves 4

8 ounces lean braised beef
8 ounces roast veal
7 ounces piece of boiled ham
7 ounces firm, smooth pork sausage
2 eating apples, peeled and cored
6 pickled gherkins
2 tablespoons capers
4 eggs, hard boiled
2 egg yolks, raw
1 teaspoon medium-hot mustard
2–3 tablespoons white wine vinegar
Salt and freshly ground pepper to taste

1. Slice the beef, veal, ham, sausage, apples, and gherkins into thin strips. Put these ingredients in a bowl and add the capers. Remove the whites from the hard-boiled eggs, dice them fine and combine with the meat mixture.

2. Mash the hard-boiled egg yolks. Using a balloon whisk, whisk the raw egg yolks and mustard into the mashed yolks. Season to taste with vinegar, salt, and pepper and continue whisking until all the ingredients are thoroughly combined.

3. Pour the dressing over the salad ingredients and toss to ensure that everything is well coated. Put the salad in the refrigerator for the flavors to combine before serving.

For a change, you can add strips of boiled beets or cold roast pork to the salad.

Potato Salad
(Kartoffelsalat)

Serves 4

2 pounds firm, waxy potatoes
1–2 onions
1 cup warm meat stock or beef broth
Salt and freshly ground pepper to taste
4–6 tablespoons white wine vinegar
5 ounces bacon
1 bunch of fresh chives

1. Wash the potatoes. Bring a saucepan of water to a boil, add the potatoes, and cook until just tender. Strain the potatoes, leave to cool, then peel them. Slice the potatoes thinly and put them in a bowl.

2. Peel and dice the onions and add them to the potatoes.

3. Whisk the warm meat stock together with the salt, pepper, and vinegar to taste. Pour the mixture over the potatoes and onions and mix well. Leave to infuse for about 15 minutes.

4. Chop the bacon finely and fry it in a skillet over a medium heat until crisp. Pour the bacon and fat over the salad immediately and mix everything together well. Transfer to a serving dish.

5. Chop the fresh chives finely and serve the salad warm, garnished with the chives.

With this type of potato salad it doesn't matter if the potatoes crumble a little when you slice them, but you must use a firm, waxy potato that won't go too soft when boiled.

Marinated Cheese
(Handkäs mit Musik)

Serves 4

14 ounces of Monterey Jack cheese, or other
strong-flavored cheddar cheese
2 onions
2–3 tablespoons white wine vinegar
Salt and freshly ground pepper to taste
3–5 tablespoons corn oil
1 bunch of fresh chives

1. Slice the cheese ¼ inch thick and layer the
slices in a shallow dish.

2. Peel the onions and slice very thin,
preferably on a mandolin. Scatter the onion
rings over the cheese.

3. Whisk the vinegar, salt, pepper, and a little
water together, then add the oil, whisking all
the time.

4. Pour the marinade over the cheese and
onions and leave to marinate for at least
1 hour.

5. Finely chop the chives and sprinkle them
over the cheese. Serve with freshly baked
whole wheat or whole grain bread and butter,
or crisp pretzels.

*Low-fat hard cheese is a perfect supper for
warm summer evenings. The salad contains
lots of protein, is low in calories and, when
dressed with vinegar and corn oil, tastes
wonderfully refreshing.*

Cheese Spread
(Obatzda)

Serves 4

7 ounces ripe Camembert, softened
⅓ cup + 1½ tablespoons butter, softened
1 small onion
Sweet paprika
Freshly ground pepper
Pinch of ground caraway
Pinch of salt
1 tablespoon finely chopped fresh chives
(optional)

1. Cut the cheese and the butter into small
pieces, then mash them together with a fork to
form a paste.

2. Peel the onion, chop finely, and fold into
the cheese and butter mixture. Beat it until a
creamy, but not too smooth, mixture forms.

3. Season the mixture well with paprika,
pepper, caraway, and a little salt. Sprinkle
with the finely chopped chives, if used. Serve
with radishes and tasty whole wheat bread.

The Bavarian German dialect name Obatzda
is difficult to translate. Batzen *equates to*
patzen *(botch, splotch) in standard German,
but also includes an element that implies
kneading.* Obatzda *is also a type of "kneaded"
Camembert. This Bavarian specialty is an
essential part of any Bavarian beer garden
snack. This recipe is for the original version.*

Bacon, Onion, and Mushroom Quiche
(Schinkenkuchen)

Serves 4

<u>For the pastry:</u>
I cup all-purpose flour, Pinch of salt to taste, I cup butter
I cup cream cheese, well chilled
Dried peas or beans, or pie weights for baking blind
<u>For the filling:</u>
4 tablespoons breadcrumbs, 4 ounces bacon, chopped
2 large onions, 7 ounce piece of boiled ham, 6 ounces mushrooms,
2 teaspoons butter, 4 eggs, ⅔ cup Cheddar cheese, freshly grated
Salt and freshly ground pepper to taste, Freshly grated nutmeg to taste
¾ cup crème fraîche

1. To make the pastry: Put the flour and salt in a bowl, rub the butter into the flour until it resembles fine breadcrumbs, add the cream cheese, cut into small pieces, to the flour, and quickly work the ingredients together to form a smooth dough. Wrap the pastry in plastic wrap and allow it to rest in the refrigerator for 30 minutes. Roll out the pastry into an oblong, then fold one third of the pastry into the middle, fold the opposite third over it to form an envelope. The end result should be three equal layers on top of each other. Cover the pastry and let it rest for 10 minutes.

2. Preheat the oven to 400°F. Divide the pastry in half. Roll out each portion on a floured board or work surface until about ⅛ inch thick. Use each sheet of pastry to line a quiche tin, approximately 9 inches in diameter.

3. To prevent the pastry from rising and the sides shrinking, the pastry should be baked blind. Place a sheet of aluminum foil over each base and cover it with dried peas, beans, or pie weights. Bake for 15–20 minutes.

4. Remove the beans or weights and the foil from the pastry cases and sprinkle the breadcrumbs and chopped bacon over the bases.

5. Peel and dice the onions. Finely dice the boiled ham. Wipe the mushrooms and slice them thin. Melt the butter in a skillet and sauté the mushrooms until just soft. Beat the eggs and fold in the diced onion, diced ham, sliced mushrooms, and grated cheese. Season with salt, pepper, and grated nutmeg, and divide the mixture equally between the prepared pastry cases. Spread the crème fraîche over the egg mixture.

6. Bake the quiches on the middle shelf of the oven for 30 minutes. Serve hot.

This quiche tastes delicious fresh from the oven, with a salad as a light meal, or at room temperature, with a glass of wine.

Spinach Soufflé with Butter Sauce
(Spinatpudding mit Buttersauce)

Serves 4

<u>For the spinach soufflé:</u>
3 handfuls fresh, young spinach leaves
Salt and freshly ground pepper to taste
6 eggs, separated, 2–3 slices good, white bread, crusts removed
½ cup milk, 1 onion, 8 teaspoons butter, 2 ounce piece of boiled ham, diced
Butter and breadcrumbs for the soufflé dish
<u>For the butter sauce:</u>
5 tablespoons butter, 2¼ tablespoons all-purpose flour
½–1 cup boiling meat stock, 1 egg yolk
Salt to taste, A squeeze of lemon juice

1. Carefully pick over the spinach and wash it thoroughly. Bring a saucepan of salted water to a boil, put the spinach in the boiling water and blanch it quickly. Refresh it in ice-cold water and drain it well.

2. Whisk the egg whites until very stiff and refrigerate them. Break the bread slices into pieces and soak in the milk to soften.

3. Peel the onion. Finely chop the onion and spinach leaves. Melt the butter in a saucepan and sweat the chopped onion and spinach. Drain the bread, squeeze out the milk, and add the pieces of the bread to the spinach and onions. Gradually beat the egg yolks and diced ham into the spinach mixture. Remove the saucepan from the heat, season the mixture with salt and pepper, and carefully fold the well-chilled egg whites into the spinach mixture.

4. Grease a soufflé dish with butter and dust it with breadcrumbs. Transfer the spinach mixture to the soufflé dish. Stand the soufflé dish in a roasting pan and fill the pan with hot water until it comes about half way up the side of the soufflé dish. Bake the soufflé for about 1 hour at 375°F. Check occasionally to make sure the water does not evaporate, and top up as necessary.

5. While the soufflé is cooking, melt the butter for the sauce in a saucepan, stir the flour into it, and cook for a minute or two. Add the boiling meat stock slowly, stirring all the time, let the sauce thicken, and beat it until light and creamy. Enrich the sauce with the egg yolk and season to taste with a little salt and lemon juice. The sauce should taste slightly lemony.

6. Take the soufflé out of the oven and serve it immediately. Serve the butter sauce separately.

The sauce should be fairly thick. Try adding just a little stock at first and then gradually adding more to achieve the desired consistency.

Herb Dressing
(Kräutersauce)

Serves 4

2 slices good, white bread, crusts removed
2 eggs
1 egg yolk
2–4 tablespoons olive oil
Mixed fresh herbs (e.g., chives, parsley, basil, tarragon, lemon thyme, borage, and sage) to taste
Salt and freshly ground pepper to taste
1 tablespoon white wine vinegar

1. Put the bread in a dish with some cold water and leave it to soak.

2. Using a hand-held electric mixer, beat the whole eggs and egg yolk together. Drain the bread and squeeze out the water. Break the bread into pieces and gradually add them to the egg mixture, beating all the time. Slowly trickle the olive oil into the mixture, beating constantly, until the olive oil is used up and the dressing achieves a smooth, creamy consistency.

3. Wash the herbs, pat them dry and strip off the leaves. Finely chop the leaves and stir them into the dressing. Season the dressing to taste with salt, pepper, and vinegar.

You can prepare your favorite herb dressing using the same method. You can use just chives, for example, or parsley. A little finely minced garlic will add more zip to the dressing.

Vinaigrette Dressing
(Sauce Vinaigrette)

Serves 4

1 egg, hard boiled
2 teaspoons hot mustard
6 tablespoons corn oil
1 onion
2 tablespoons finely chopped mixed fresh herbs
4 tablespoons balsamic vinegar
2 tablespoons red wine
Salt and freshly ground pepper to taste
Pinch of sugar to taste

1. Mash the hard-boiled egg with a fork until very smooth. Add the mustard to the mashed egg and mix them together. Using a small balloon whisk, whisk 2 tablespoons of the oil into the egg and mustard mixture until completely emulsified.

2. Peel and finely dice the onion. Stir the diced onion into the dressing with the chopped herbs, then gradually whisk in the vinegar, red wine, and remaining oil.

3. Season the dressing to taste with salt, pepper, and sugar.

The vinaigrette takes on a darker color due to the addition of balsamic vinegar. If I need a paler sauce, I use either champagne vinegar or white wine vinegar. You can give the dressing a very special flavor by using three different types of vinegar, for example balsamic vinegar, a white herb vinegar, and a little sherry vinegar.

Mayonnaise
(Mayonnaise)

Serves 4

2 egg yolks
I cup olive oil
I teaspoon medium-hot mustard
Splash of lemon juice
Splash of tarragon vinegar
Salt and freshly ground white pepper to taste

1. Put the egg yolks into a small bowl, add 1 tablespoon of the olive oil and beat the mixture with a hand-held electric mixer until foaming.

2. Add the mustard, lemon juice, a little tarragon vinegar to taste, and salt and pepper to the emulsion. Then beat in the remaining olive oil, drop by drop at first, then in a slow trickle. Continue beating until the mayonnaise is thick and creamy.

Mayonnaise can be prepared very quickly and easily using a hand-held electric mixer or a blender.
Mayonnaise prepared with corn oil is more easily digestible. If you still find it indigestible, try using the Cold Butter Sauce from the recipe on page 30.

Sauce à la Bourguignonne
(Sauce à la Bourguignonne)

Serves 4

4 large eating apples
4 large onions
6 tablespoons small capers
7–10 pickled gherkins, depending on size
Double recipe Mayonnaise (see recipe opposite)
1–2 tablespoons curry powder
Salt to taste

1. Peel, halve, and core the apples. Peel the onions. Dice 3 apples and 3 onions. Put the diced onions and apples in the bowl of a food processor with 4 tablespoons of the capers and 6 of the gherkins and purée the ingredients until smooth.

2. Dice the remaining apple, onion, and gherkins very fine and fold them into the purée along with the remaining capers.

3. Prepare the mayonnaise according to the previous recipe. Stir the purée into the mayonnaise and season to taste with curry powder and salt. The flavor should be quite hot. Cover and refrigerate for at least 4 hours, or preferably overnight, for the flavors to combine.

Aioli
(Aioli)

Serves 4

1 egg yolk
1 teaspoon mustard
4–8 cloves of garlic, to taste
Pinch of sea salt to taste
½ cup olive oil
Freshly ground black pepper to taste
Cayenne pepper to taste
Splash of lemon juice

1. Whisk the egg yolk and mustard together until creamy, using a balloon whisk.

2. Peel the cloves of garlic, chop them, and crush them with the sea salt using a mortar and pestle. Stir the garlic into the egg and mustard mixture. Add the olive oil to the dressing, drop by drop at first, then in a slow trickle, whisking all the time.

3. Season the garlic mayonnaise to taste with pepper, cayenne, and a little lemon juice.

Spicy aioli is a superb accompaniment for grilled fish. You should only use very fresh garlic for the mayonnaise to get the full aromatic flavor.

Cumberland Sauce
(Cumberlandsauce)

Serves 4

2 oranges
8 ounces cranberry relish or conserve
8 ounces redcurrant jelly
¾ cup cognac
¾ cup Cointreau
1 teaspoon ground ginger
Chili sauce or Tabasco to taste

1. Peel the oranges, remove the white pith from the rind, and cut the peel into very fine strips (julienne). Bring a saucepan of water to the boil and blanch the orange peel in the boiling water for a few seconds. Drain and refresh it in cold water.

2. Squeeze the juice from the oranges and mix it with the cranberries, redcurrant jelly, cognac, Cointreau, and ground ginger. Then fold in the orange peel.

3. Season to taste with chili sauce or Tabasco, cover, and refrigerate for at least 6 hours for the flavors to combine.

Cumberland sauce is the classic sauce for all game dishes. Of course it tastes best of all if you use cranberries that you have preserved and red currant jelly you have made yourself.

Cold Butter Sauce
(Kalte Buttersauce)

Serves 4

2 eggs, hard boiled
6½ tablespoons butter, softened
I small shallot
I tablespoon chopped fresh parsley
I tablespoon chopped fresh dill
I teaspoon chopped capers
Splash of white wine vinegar
Salt and freshly ground white pepper to taste

1. Shell the eggs, cut them in half, and scoop out the yolks. Push the yolks through a sieve. Add the butter to the sieved egg yolks and beat with a hand-held electric mixer until light and fluffy.

2. Peel the shallot and chop it fine. Chop the egg white. Add the finely chopped egg white and shallot to the butter mixture along with the chopped herbs and the capers, and beat again until light and fluffy. The sauce should be creamy and smooth.

3. Season to taste with vinegar, salt, and pepper. Refrigerate until needed.

I particularly like serving this sauce with freshly cooked asparagus, but it may be served with any dish that can be accompanied by mayonnaise.
You can, of course, add different herbs. We like the sauce when it is flavored with just chives, for example.

Avocado Dressing
(Avocadosauce)

Serves 4

2 fully ripe avocados
3–4 tablespoons lemon juice
4 tablespoons dry white wine
½ cup heavy cream
Salt and freshly ground pepper to taste
I teaspoon Worcestershire sauce
I tablespoon chopped fresh parsley (optional)

1. Peel and halve the avocados, remove the stone and mash the flesh with a fork until smooth. Add the lemon juice and white wine.

2. Whip the cream until stiff and fold it into the avocado purée. Season to taste with salt, pepper, and Worcestershire sauce.

3. The dressing looks particularly appetizing if garnished with fresh, chopped parsley. Serve it immediately, because the attractive green dressing discolors quickly.

This dressing tastes superb with steaks and schnitzel.
You should only use fully ripe avocados for the dressing. The flesh should give slightly when you press the fruit.

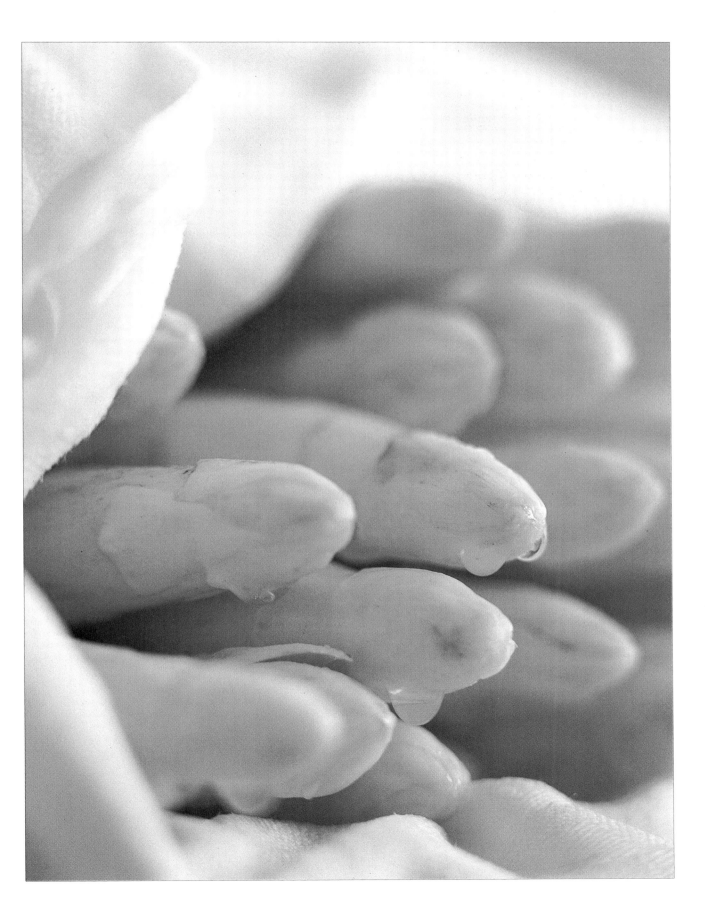

Boiled Celeriac Salad
(Gekochter Selleriesalat)

Serves 4

3 small celeriac (with leaves)
I small onion
3–4 tablespoons white wine vinegar
Salt and freshly ground pepper to taste
4 tablespoons corn oil

1. Cut off the leaves from the celeriac. Reserve the tender, young leaves. Don't throw the remaining leaves away, because they can be used to flavor soups and stews. Scrub the celeriac thoroughly, with a brush, under cold running water. Bring a saucepan of salted water to a boil, add the celeriac to the pan, and cook them for 35–40 minutes until tender.

2. Remove the celeriac from the water with a slotted spoon, and immerse them in cold water. Allow the celeriac to cool a little, then peel them. Reserve a few tablespoons of the cooking liquid.

3. While the celeriac are still warm, slice them 1 inch thick using a decorating knife. Layer the slices in a deep platter. Peel the onion, dice it fine, and scatter it over the slices of celeriac.

4. Whisk the vinegar, salt, and pepper together with a little of the cooking liquid from the celeriac, whisk in the oil, and pour the dressing over the celeriac. Leave the salad for at least one hour, so the flavors can combine.

If you like, you can chop the reserved young celeriac leaves, and scatter them over the salad.

Raw Celeriac Salad
(Roher Selleriesalat)

Serves 4

2 small celeriac (with leaves)
Juice of ½ lemon
2 ripe apples (preferably Cox Orange Pippin), peeled and cored
I small onion
Splash of walnut oil or cream
Salt and sugar to taste
Splash of lemon juice to taste (optional)

1. Remove the leaves from the celeriac. Don't throw the leaves away, because they can be used to flavor soups and stews. Scrub the celeriac thoroughly, with a brush, under cold running water, then peel them.

2. Grate the celeriac fine. Pour the lemon juice over the grated celeriac immediately, so that it does not discolor.

3. Grate the apples, and mix the grated apple into the grated celeriac. Peel and dice the onion, and add it to the grated apple and celeriac mixture.

4. Stir in the walnut oil, or cream, to the grated celeriac mixture, and season to taste with salt and sugar. You can also add more lemon juice to taste.

You can prepare a crisp salad in the same way using grated carrot or a julienne of zucchini.

Coleslaw and Bacon Salad

(Weißkrautsalat)

Serves 4

1 small white cabbage
Salt to taste
1 large onion
5–7 ounces bacon
2 tablespoons goose fat or dripping
3–4 tablespoons white wine vinegar, warmed
Salt and freshly ground pepper to taste
Ground caraway to taste

1. Remove the outer leaves from the head of cabbage, cut the cabbage into quarters, and cut out the solid heart. Slice the cabbage very thin, or grate it, and put it in a large bowl.

2. Sprinkle the salt over the cabbage, and either knead it by hand, or mash it with a large pestle, until the strips of cabbage are soft. Peel the onion, dice it, and add it to the cabbage.

3. Chop the bacon. Heat a skillet, and fry the bacon until translucent. Add the goose fat, or dripping, to the skillet and let it melt. Add the bacon, goose fat, and warmed vinegar to the cabbage mixture, and combine them thoroughly.

4. Season the salad well with the salt, pepper, and caraway, mix it well again, and leave it for several hours, at room temperature, for the flavors to combine.

Not only does the goose fat make the cabbage salad glisten, it also tastes delicious.

Kohlrabi Salad

(Kohlrabisalat)

Serves 4

4 medium-sized kohlrabi
Salt to taste
2–3 tablespoons white wine vinegar
2–3 tablespoons corn oil

1. Remove the leaves from the kohlrabi, reserving the tender, young leaves. Peel and dice the kohlrabi. Bring a saucepan of salted water to a boil, and cook the kohlrabi in it until *al dente*. Drain them in a colander, reserving ½ cup of the cooking liquid. Put the kohlrabi into a shallow dish.

2. Whisk together the reserved cooking liquid, salt, vinegar, and corn oil. Pour it over the kohlrabi, and marinate the salad in the dressing. Allow the flavors to combine, and serve at room temperature.

3. Finely chop the reserved kohlrabi leaves, and sprinkle them over the salad.

Cauliflower or broccoli salad can be prepared in the same way.

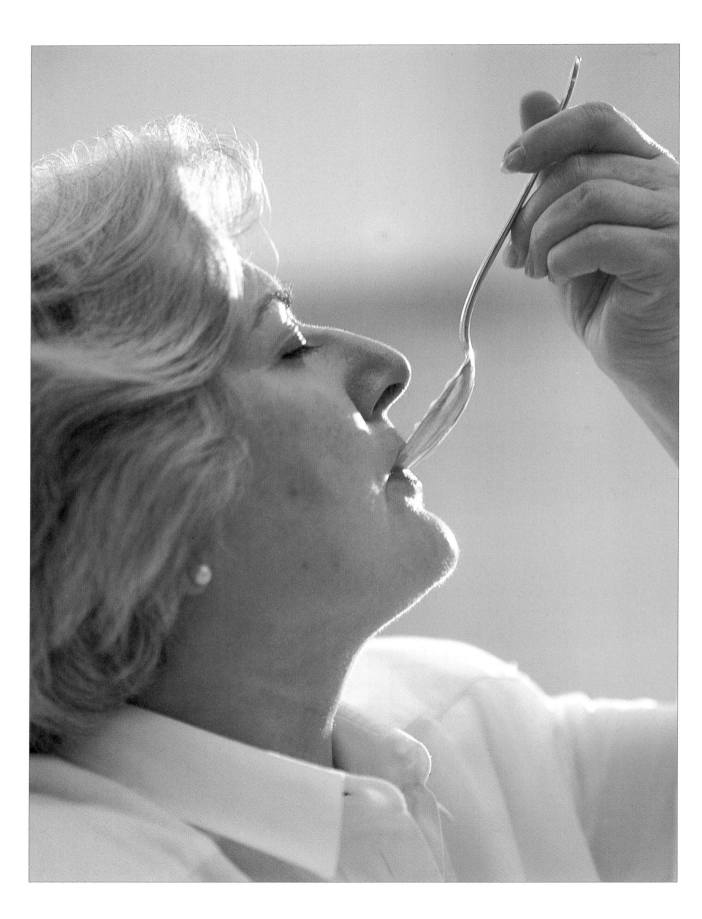

A steaming bowl of soup is delicious at any time of day.
A smooth porridge can provide a gentle start to the day for a
sensitive stomach. At lunchtime, a strong beef broth takes the
edge off your hunger if you haven't got time to cook. Personally,
I don't think I've missed out if all I have for lunch is a hearty soup and
a small dessert. Beef broth enriched with egg yolk is particularly
beneficial at the end of a stressful day. And spicy soup can help revive
you after one drink too many at a celebration. In short, soup keeps
body and soul together.

My mother always cooked a stew on Saturdays. Sometimes it
contained a lot of meat, sometimes only a little, but there was
always enough left over for the following Monday. In the past,
Monday was always wash day and, before the advent of washing
machines, a hard working day for every housewife. It made life
easier for everyone if dinner had been cooked in advance.
As children, we certainly didn't turn up our noses at eating the
leftovers, quite the contrary, because almost all soups and
stews taste better when reheated.

I have passed on my love of stews and soups to my family,
so I always ensure that I have beef, veal, or vegetable stock in the freezer.
If I don't have time to cook, the whole family is happy with,
and satisfied by, a steaming bowl of soup, enriched with noodles or beaten egg.

Beef Consommé, Beef Tea, Beef and Veal Stock

(Fleischbrühe, Kraftbrühe, Rinder- und Kalbsfond)

Serves 4–6

For the beef stock:
1 handful of beef bones, for making soup
2 marrow bones, 1 piece of beef liver
1 large carrot, 1 parsley root
1 thin leek, ¼ celeriac, ½ bunch fresh parsley
1¾ pounds piece of chuck or rib steak, 1 tablespoon salt

1. Wash the beef bones and marrow bones under cold, running water and put them in a stock pot along with the beef liver. Add 12½ cups of cold water and bring the stock pot to a boil.

2. Wash the vegetables. Peel and chop the carrot, parsley root, and celeriac, slice the leek, and add the vegetables to the boiling stock with the parsley and the piece of chuck, or rib steak. Season with salt and simmer over a low heat for 2½ hours.

3. When the meat is tender, pour a little cold water into the stock. This is my tip for a fast way to clarify stock. You can, however, also use the method described on page 21, in the recipe for Beef Brawn.

4. Remove the meat from the stock pot and use it for another recipe. Strain the stock carefully through a fine sieve and allow it to cool. This way the fat rises to the surface, and sets, so it is easier to remove it from the stock.

Variations:

• If you want to make beef tea, bring the stock to a boil, and reduce it until it reaches the desired strength.

• Veal stock is prepared in the same way, using 1 pound bones from the veal cutlets, or loin, 8 ounces chopped veal shoulder, 1 carrot, 1 parsley root, 1 bunch of fresh parsley.

• To make beef consommé, finely dice 1–1¾ pounds very lean beef. Make a bouquet garni using 1 finely chopped onion, 1 finely chopped carrot, and 4–5 peppercorns. Put them in a cheesecloth bag, and add them to the stock pot with the beef. Add enough cold water to cover the meat. Bring the stock pot to a boil, and simmer it over a medium heat, until the beef is tender. Drain off the stock, stir in 1–2 beaten egg yolks, and serve. This beef consommé is good enough to "raise the dead"!

The boiled chuck or rib steak tastes good as a main meal, when served with a little of the stock poured over it. To me and my family, bone marrow spread on pumpernickel bread, and sprinkled with a little salt, is a real delicacy. The inclusion of liver in the stock is not to everyone's taste, so it can be omitted.

Clear Chicken Consommé
(Klare Hühnerbrühe)

Serves 4

2 pounds chicken parts, or 1 whole chicken,
weighing about 2 pounds
1 large onion, peeled
2 cloves
1 large carrot, peeled and finely chopped
4–5 peppercorns
1 teaspoon salt

1. Wash the chicken joints, or whole chicken, and remove any visible fat. Spike the onion with the cloves. Put the chicken, carrot, onion, peppercorns, and the salt in a large saucepan, or stock pot, and cover with 12½ cups of cold water. Bring the saucepan to a boil and simmer until the chicken is tender.

2. Remove the chicken joints, or whole chicken, and allow it to cool a little. Take the chicken meat off the bone, chop it fine, and use it in soup, or to make the Chicken Stew on page 49.

3. Strain the consommé through a sieve, and refrigerate it overnight. Next day, remove the fat that will have set on top of the broth. Reheat the consommé, and serve it with the garnish of your choice (see pages 38–40), or reduce it to a rich stock.

I always cook a chicken in a pressure cooker for 20 minutes, then take the pan off the heat and allow the chicken to finish cooking.

Clear Vegetable Consommé
(Klare Gemüsebrühe)

Serves 4

1 onion, outer layer of skin removed
2 cloves
3–4 carrots, peeled and roughly chopped
1 celeriac, peeled and roughly chopped
2 leeks, sliced
2 parsley roots, peeled and roughly chopped
1 bunch fresh parsley
½ bunch fresh dill
5–6 peppercorns
Selection of seasonal vegetables
(e.g. green beans, tomatoes, zucchini)

1. Spike the onion with the cloves. Put the chopped vegetables in a large saucepan, or stock pot, with the onion, parsley, dill, and peppercorns, and cover the vegetables with plenty of water. Prepare the seasonal vegetables, chop them fine, add them to the saucepan, and bring to a boil. Reduce the heat and boil gently until the vegetables are tender.

2. Strain the vegetable consommé and discard the vegetables. Serve the hot consommé with the garnish of your choice (see pages 38–40), or reduce to a rich stock.

I also prefer cooking the vegetable consommé in a pressure cooker. Bring the pressure cooker up to pressure and steam for 15 minutes, then remove the pan from the heat and allow the vegetables to finish cooking. The brown onion skin lends the vegetable consommé a very attractive color.

Semolina Dumplings
(Schwemmklößchen)

Serves 4

¼ cup butter, softened
2 eggs, beaten
½ cup semolina
Salt to taste
Freshly grated nutmeg to taste
Broth or consommé

1. Beat the softened butter until creamy, and alternately add small quantities of beaten eggs, and semolina, stirring them in thoroughly each time. Season generously with salt and nutmeg.

2. Allow the batter to rest for 15 minutes.

3. Using two damp teaspoons, shape spoonfuls of the batter into little dumplings. Bring a saucepan of salted water to a boil, and drop the dumplings into the simmering water. Cook the dumplings in the simmering water for about 10 minutes, until they swell and float to the top of the pan.

4. Scoop the dumplings out of the water with a slotted spoon and refresh them in ice-cold water. Put the broth or consommé in a saucepan and bring it to a boil. Transfer the dumplings to the hot broth or consommé and continue to cook them for a few minutes. The dumplings should have doubled in size.

The precise quantity of semolina depends on the size of the eggs, so you may need to use a little more than stated in the recipe. You should use durum wheat semolina, as this helps the dumplings to keep their shape when cooked.

Choux Pastry Dumplings
(Brandteigknödelchen)

Serves 4

1 cup whole milk
5 tablespoons butter
Salt and freshly grated nutmeg to taste
⅔ cup all-purpose flour
2 eggs
3 egg yolks, beaten
Corn oil for frying
Broth or consommé

1. Put the milk, butter, salt, and nutmeg in a saucepan, and bring the mixture to a boil. Add all the flour, beat the mixture constantly with a wooden spoon, until all the flour is incorporated, the dough comes away from the base and sides of the saucepan, and forms a soft ball.

2. Take the saucepan off the heat, and allow the dough to cool a little. Beat in the whole eggs, one at a time, then gradually beat in the egg yolks.

3. Heat the oil in a deep saucepan, or deep-fat fryer. Using a teaspoon, shape the batter into small dumplings, and drop them into the hot oil. Fry the dumplings until they are golden brown. Take the dumplings out of the hot oil, using a slotted spoon and drain them on absorbent kitchen paper. Put the broth or consommé in a saucepan and bring it to a boil. Just before the broth or consommé is ready to serve, garnish it with the dumplings, so they stay crisp.

If you want to make a sweet choux pastry, add 6½ tablespoons sugar, just a small pinch of salt, and omit the nutmeg.

Bone Marrow Dumplings
(Markklößchen)

Serves 4

1½ ounces beef bone marrow
2 eggs, beaten
5–6 tablespoons fresh breadcrumbs
1 tablespoon chopped fresh parsley
1 tablespoon diced onion
Pinch of grated lemon zest to taste
Salt and freshly grated nutmeg to taste
Beef broth or consommé

1. Soak the bone marrow in cold water, so that it turns white. Drain the bone marrow, transfer it to a saucepan, and heat it gently for a few minutes.

2. Mash the bone marrow with a fork, then beat it with a balloon whisk, until it is very light and fluffy. Gradually fold in the beaten eggs, breadcrumbs, parsley, and diced onion, season with the lemon zest, salt, and nutmeg, and allow the mixture to rest for about 30 minutes.

3. Put the broth, or consommé, in a saucepan, and bring it to a boil, then reduce the heat so that it is simmering gently. Shape the bone marrow mixture into hazelnut-sized dumplings, and drop them into the simmering broth. Bring the broth to a boil again, reduce the heat, and simmer the dumplings for about 15 minutes.

If the batter is too stiff, stir one tablespoon of the hot broth into it, so it becomes malleable again.

Liver Spätzle
(Leberspätzle)

Serves 4

3 tablespoons butter, softened
1 egg, beaten
5–6 tablespoons fresh breadcrumbs
3–4 tablespoons whole milk
3–4 ounces calf's liver, finely chopped
1 tablespoon chopped fresh parsley
1 teaspoon diced onion
Pinch of dried, rubbed marjoram to taste
Grated zest of ½ lemon
Salt and freshly ground pepper to taste
Beef broth or consommé

1. Put the softened butter in a bowl, add the beaten egg, and beat them together until creamy. Soak the breadcrumbs in the milk. Alternately stir a small amount of the moistened breadcrumbs, chopped liver, chopped parsley, and diced onion into the butter mixture. Season with the marjoram, lemon zest, salt, and pepper. Allow the flavors to combine.

2. Put the broth, or consommé, in a saucepan, bring it to a boil, then reduce the heat until it is simmering gently. Push the liver mixture through a potato ricer over the pan of simmering broth. When all the liver mixture has been used, quickly bring the broth to a boil again, and simmer it for a few minutes. Serve it immediately.

Beef Meatballs
(Fleischknödel)

Serves 4

1 stale bread roll
⅓ cup + 1½ tablespoons whole milk, or water
3 tablespoons butter, softened
1 egg, beaten
5 ounces ground lean beef
1 teaspoon chopped fresh parsley
1 teaspoon diced onion
Grated zest of ½ lemon
Salt and freshly ground pepper to taste
Beef broth or consommé

1. Grate the crust off the bread roll and soak the bread in the milk, or water, for about 10 minutes.

2. Beat together the softened butter and beaten egg until creamy. Squeeze the milk, or water, out of the bread roll, break it into small pieces, and gradually beat them into the butter mixture.

3. Add the ground beef, chopped parsley, and diced onion to the bread mixture, and beat it until a smooth mixture forms. Season with the lemon zest, salt, and pepper.

4. Dampen your hands, and shape the meat mixture into small meatballs. Put the broth, or consommé, in a saucepan, bring it to a boil, then reduce the heat until the broth is simmering gently. Place the meatballs in the simmering broth. Bring the broth to a boil again, reduce it to a simmer, and cook the meatballs for about 15 minutes.

Sponge Garnish
(Suppenbiskuit)

Serves 4

½ cup butter, softened
1½ cups all-purpose flour
6 eggs
Butter to grease the baking pan
Salt to taste

1. Using a hand-held electric mixer, beat the softened butter until very light and creamy. Alternately beat in some of the flour, then the eggs, one at a time, until both flour and eggs are used up. Season with salt.

2. Preheat the oven to 350°F. Grease a small, square, baking pan. Pour the mixture into the pan, and bake in the center of the oven until the cake is golden-brown and the edges have come away slightly from the sides of the pan.

3. Turn the cake out onto a wire rack. Allow it to cool, then cut it into small squares.

This garnish is delicious in a strong, clear vegetable consommé. The soup looks even more appetizing if it is also garnished with a julienne of carrots and leeks. The sponge squares will keep for about two weeks if stored in an airtight tin, in a cool place.

Fresh Pea Soup
(Erbsensuppe aus frischen Erbsen)

Serves 4

3 tablespoons butter, 2 onions, peeled and finely diced
1 pound fresh peas, shelled, 2 cups meat stock
13 tablespoons crème fraîche
2 tablespoons white wine, Salt and freshly ground pepper to taste
Mint or watercress, finely chopped, Frankfurters (optional)

1. Melt the butter in a saucepan, and fry the diced onion in it, until it is translucent.

2. Add half the shelled peas to the saucepan, and soften them in the butter. Add the stock, and quickly bring it to a boil. Stir in the crème fraîche, add the white wine, and simmer the soup over a low heat for 10 minutes until the peas are tender.

3. Season with salt and pepper. Purée the soup with a hand-held electric blender until smooth.

4. Stir the remaining peas into the soup, and simmer gently until tender. Divide the soup equally between four plates. Garnish each plate with a sprinkling of chopped mint or watercress.

5. If you like, you can serve the soup with a couple of hot frankfurters per person.

I often prepare this soup with frozen peas.

Tomato Soup
(Tomatensuppe)

Serves 4

2 pounds ripe tomatoes
I large, floury potato
Salt and freshly ground pepper to taste
I cup heavy cream
2 slices of stale white bread, crusts removed
½ stick butter
8–10 leaves fresh basil, cut into ribbons

1. Remove the stalks from the tomatoes. Wash and chop the tomatoes. Peel and grate the potato. Put the chopped tomatoes and grated potato in a saucepan. Add enough cold water to cover them, season with salt and pepper, and bring to a boil. Simmer over a medium heat, until soft.

2. In the meantime, whip half the cream until it stands in soft peaks. Take care not to over whip it. Cover and refrigerate.

3. Pass the tomato and potato mixture through a fine sieve, then reheat the purée. Stir in the remaining cream and adjust the seasoning to taste.

4. Cut the bread slices into small cubes. Melt the butter in a skillet, and sauté the cubes in the butter until golden brown and crisp. Remove the croutons from the skillet, and drain them on absorbent kitchen paper.

5. Fold the whipped cream into the tomato soup. Divide the soup equally between warmed soup plates, and garnish it with the ribbons of basil and the croutons.

Cream of Pepper Soup
(Paprikacremesuppe)

Serves 4

5 tablespoons corn oil
2 medium carrots, peeled and finely chopped
2 medium onions, peeled and finely chopped
I small celeriac, peeled and finely chopped
4¼ cups chicken stock
2 floury potatoes, peeled and grated
2 large, yellow peppers, halved, seeded and finely chopped
¾ cup light cream
2 slices white bread, crusts removed
I–2 tablespoons freshly grated parmesan

1. Heat 2 tablespoons of the oil in a saucepan, and fry the chopped carrots, onions, and celeriac. Add the chicken stock and bring it to a boil.

2. Add the grated potato and chopped peppers to the boiling soup. Reduce the heat and simmer until the vegetables are soft.

3. Push the soup through a fine sieve and reheat the resulting purée. Fold in the cream and let it combine with the soup.

4. Heat the remaining 3 tablespoons of oil in a skillet. Cut the slices of bread into small cubes, then sauté them in the oil until golden brown and crisp.

5. Divide the soup equally between four warmed plates. Garnish with the croutons and freshly grated parmesan.

Game Soup
(Schwarzwildbretsuppe)

Serves 4

8 teaspoons clarified butter
3½ tablespoons all-purpose flour
2 teaspoons sugar
1 tablespoon diced onion
5 juniper berries, crushed
3 cloves
3 bay leaves
Pinch of salt to taste
4½ cups hot beef stock
1 tablespoon white wine vinegar
1 tablespoon lemon juice
Grated zest of 1 lemon
4 ounces cold, roast game, diced
Splash of Madeira wine

1. Melt the clarified butter in a saucepan, add the flour, and cook it gently in the butter, stirring all the time, until it turns golden brown. Add the sugar and let it caramelize.

2. Add the diced onion, crushed juniper berries, cloves, bay leaves, and the salt, then add the hot stock, stirring constantly. Season the soup with the vinegar, lemon juice, and lemon zest, and allow the flavors to infuse thoroughly.

3. Put the diced, roast game into another saucepan, strain the soup through a sieve and pour it over the game. Bring the soup to a boil again, and flavor the soup with a splash of Madeira, if liked.

This basic recipe is ideally suited to using up all kinds of leftover dark meat.

Belgian Endive Soup
(Endiviensuppe)

Serves 4

1 Belgian endive
8 teaspoons butter
3½ tablespoons all-purpose flour
2–3 cups hot beef stock
Pinch of salt to taste
Splash of milk to taste
Fresh watercress to garnish

1. Wash the endive, drain it well, cut it in half, then cut each half into ribbons.

2. Melt the butter in a saucepan, and sweat the endive in it.

3. Sprinkle the flour over the endive. Cook it gently, stirring all the time, until the flour turns golden, then add the hot beef stock. Bring the soup to a boil, stirring constantly. Simmer it for a few minutes, and season with salt, if necessary.

4. Just before serving, enrich the soup with a splash of milk. Divide the soup equally between four heated plates and garnish with watercress.

The finer you slice the endive, the creamier the soup. Instead of endive, you can also use samphire, or chervil, for this soup. Chop two handfuls of your chosen herb very fine, and prepare the soup in the same way. Garnish with the same chopped herb as you have used in your soup, rather than with watercress.

Potato Soup with Trout Caviar

(Kartoffelsuppe mit Forellenkaviar)

Serves 4

8 teaspoons butter
4–6 large, baking potatoes, peeled and finely chopped
1 onion, peeled and finely chopped
1 large carrot, peeled and finely chopped
1 large parsley root, peeled and finely chopped
¼ celeriac, peeled and finely chopped
3 cups hot meat stock
Salt and freshly ground pepper to taste
Pinch of dried, rubbed marjoram
½ cup heavy cream, whipped
3 tablespoons trout caviar

1. Melt the butter in a saucepan, add the chopped vegetables and sweat them gently. Add the hot meat stock and cook the vegetables until they are very soft.

2. Pass the soup through a sieve and season it with salt, pepper, and marjoram. Fold half of the whipped cream into the soup.

3. Divide the soup equally between four warmed soup plates. Garnish each plate with a teaspoon of whipped cream and a sprinkling of trout caviar.

You can also use thin strips of smoked salmon as a garnish, instead of the trout caviar.

Lower Bavarian Potato Soup

(Niederbayerische Kartoffelsuppe)

Serves 4

1 leek
1 pound baking potatoes, peeled and finely diced
2 carrots, peeled and finely diced
1 small piece celeriac, peeled and finely diced
Salt and freshly ground pepper to taste
1 tablespoon chopped fresh parsley

1. Cut the leek in half lengthways, wash it thoroughly, then cut into thin strips. Put all the vegetables in a saucepan with enough cold water to cover them. Bring the saucepan to a boil, then simmer the vegetables over a medium heat, until they are very soft.

2. Season the soup with salt and pepper. Sprinkle the chopped parsley over it before serving.

This is a typical soup for fast days. If you use a good, rich stock instead of the water, the soup is more nourishing.

Oxtail Soup
(Ochsenschwanzsuppe)

Serves 6–8

2½ pounds oxtail pieces, 1 pound lean beef (rump or silverside)
2 carrots, peeled and chopped, 1 leek, washed and sliced
2 parsley roots, peeled and chopped
1 bunch fresh parsley, chopped, 3 bay leaves
10 peppercorns, 5 juniper berries, crushed
3½ tablespoons all-purpose flour, 4 tablespoons tomato purée
Freshly ground pepper to taste, Sweet paprika to taste
Pinch of salt to taste, 2 cups robust red wine (e.g., Bordeaux, Côtes-du-Rhône)
Croutons to taste

1. Put the oxtail pieces into a large saucepan, or preferably a pressure cooker, with the beef, chopped vegetables, the parsley, bay leaves, peppercorns, and juniper berries. Add sufficient water to cover the ingredients. Bring the pan to a boil, and simmer it until the beef is tender. Strain the stock, reserving the meat. Allow the stock to cool overnight.

2. Next day, skim the fat from the stock then reheat the stock. Measure out eight teaspoons of fat skimmed from the stock and melt it in a small saucepan. Stir in the all-purpose flour, cook it until it foams, stirring constantly, then add the tomato purée.

3. Pour the hot oxtail stock onto the roux, and season it with the pepper, paprika, and salt. Bring it to a boil, stirring constantly, and then simmer on a medium heat for about 20 minutes, until the flavors have combined well.

4. Take the oxtail meat off the bones. Dice the oxtail and beef, then add the meat to the soup.

5. Finally add the red wine and bring the soup to a boil again. Serve the soup garnished with croutons (see Tomato Soup recipe on page 42).

When preparing this soup, bear in mind that it is going to be enriched with red wine. You can cook the soup well in advance, and then add the red wine when you reheat it, because this soup really tastes better when reheated. It is also perfect for freezing.

Indian Chicken Soup
(Indische Hühnersuppe)

Serves 4

1 pound chicken gizzards
Pinch of salt to taste
1 small onion, peeled
3 cloves, 1 bay leaf
1 small carrot, peeled and chopped
5–6 peppercorns, 8 teaspoons butter
2 tablespoons all-purpose flour
Juice of ½ lemon
1 egg yolk, beaten

1. Carefully wash, clean, and trim the chicken gizzards, and put them in a large saucepan. Add enough water to cover them completely, and season them with salt. Spike the onion with the cloves. Add the chopped carrot, whole onion, bay leaf, and peppercorns to the saucepan. Bring the pan to a boil and simmer it until the chicken gizzards are tender. Strain the resulting stock through a sieve, reserving the stock and gizzards.

2. Reheat the chicken stock. Melt the butter in a saucepan, then add the flour, stirring all the time. When the mixture froths, add the hot chicken stock, stirring constantly, and cook until the soup thickens. Chop the chicken gizzards and add to the soup.

3. Simmer the soup until the chopped chicken is heated through, then season generously with salt and lemon juice. Thicken the soup with the beaten egg yolk and serve immediately.

My mother-in-law got the recipe for this soup from her sister, who lives in Austria. We thought it very funny when it was recommended to us, in Bombay, as an Indian specialty.

Pumpkin Soup
(Kürbissuppe)

Serves 4

1 pound yellow pumpkin flesh,
derinded and seeded
Pinch of salt to taste
8 teaspoons butter
2 tablespoons all-purpose flour
Freshly grated nutmeg to taste
Splash of white wine vinegar

1. Dice the pumpkin flesh. Bring a saucepan of salted water to a boil, add the pumpkin flesh and cook until soft. Strain the pumpkin stock, reserving it. Set aside the pumpkin flesh and, when it is cool enough, dice into small cubes.

2. Melt the butter in a saucepan and add the flour, stirring all the time. When the flour froths, gradually add the hot pumpkin stock, stirring constantly, until a creamy soup forms. Bring the soup to a boil, then reduce the heat and simmer until it thickens.

3. Add the diced pumpkin, heat the soup through thoroughly, then purée through a sieve.

4. Reheat the soup again and season it with salt, nutmeg, and a splash of white wine vinegar. If necessary, dilute the soup with more pumpkin stock.

You can make a very wide range of vegetable soups, using the same basic golden roux. I also make asparagus soup, with a blond roux, using 8 teaspoons of butter and a heaped tablespoon of all-purpose flour. I add the stock from the boiled asparagus, and thicken the soup with a beaten egg yolk.

Pichelsteiner Stew

(Pichelsteiner)

Serves 6–8

3 medium potatoes, 3 medium carrots
5 parsley roots, 1 small celeriac
6 medium onions, 1–2 leeks
3 tablespoons chopped fresh parsley, ½ pound beef
½ pound pork (preferably shoulder), ½ pound lean lamb
2 tablespoons butter, Salt to taste
Freshly ground pepper to taste, 1 cup meat stock

1. Peel the potatoes, carrots, parsley roots, celeriac, and onions. Wash the leeks. Cut all the vegetables into medium-thick slices.

2. Rinse the meats, pat them dry, then cut them into small cubes.

3. Preheat the oven to 400°F. Grease the base of a casserole dish very well with the butter. Arrange a layer of potatoes on the base of the casserole, followed by alternate layers of the root vegetables, chopped parsley, and a layer of beef. Season it with salt and pepper to taste.

Repeat this process, layering the vegetables and parsley, with the pork and finally the lamb, finishing with a layer of potato.

4. Pour the stock over the layered casserole and cover the dish. Cook in the oven for 1½–2 hours, until the meat is tender. You should not take the lid off the casserole while it is cooking, and should only stir the stew just before serving it.

Substitute sliced mushrooms, preferably fresh porcini, for the meat and give everyone, not just vegetarians, a treat.

Chicken Stew
(Hühnereintopf)

Serves 4

1 leek, washed
3 medium carrots, peeled
8 teaspoons butter
5 cups chicken stock
Salt and freshly ground pepper to taste
½ cup vermicelli
Meat from 1 whole chicken, off the bone
2 egg yolks
6 tablespoons light cream
Grated zest of 1 lemon
1 tablespoon lemon juice
Pinch of sugar to taste

1. Slice the leek and carrots. Melt the butter in a saucepan and sweat the sliced vegetables in the butter, until soft.

2. Add the chicken stock to the pan, season with salt and pepper, then bring it to a boil.

3. Add the vermicelli to the stew, reduce the heat, and simmer for 10–15 minutes on a low heat.

4. Dice the chicken meat fine, and stir it into the stew.

5. Beat together the egg yolks, cream, lemon zest, and lemon juice. Add the egg mixture to the stew to thicken the gravy. Season it with salt, pepper, and the sugar to taste. Serve the stew immediately.

You can also use sliced, roast chicken breast for the meat.

Pea Stew
(Erbseneintopf)

Serves 4

2 cups green split peas
2 carrots
1 small piece celeriac
2–3 baking potatoes
1 small leek
½ pound lean pork or lamb
2 tablespoons corn oil
Salt and freshly ground pepper to taste
Ground caraway to taste
1 tablespoon chopped fresh parsley

1. Rinse the split peas in a colander, with plenty of running water. Peel the carrots, celeriac, and potatoes, wash the leek, then chop all the vegetables. Cut the pork, or lamb, into small cubes.

2. Heat the oil in a flameproof casserole dish on top of the stove, until very hot, then sear the meat in the hot oil. Add the split peas to the casserole dish, sweat them briefly in the hot oil. Cover well with cold water, bring up to a boil, then add the prepared vegetables. Reduce the heat and simmer for 1½–2 hours. Check the level of liquid during cooking as split peas are very absorbent.

3. Season the stew with salt, pepper, and caraway. Stir the chopped parsley into the stew just before serving.

It doesn't matter if this stew overcooks a bit, because this way it develops its full flavor. I also prepare lentil, or bean stews, in the same way.

*N*ot everyone in my family shares my love of fish.
The bones do cause problems, once in a while. Personally,
I have enjoyed eating fish all my life, and have therefore compiled
both very simple and rather more complicated recipes.

Pike quenelles, or a fish soufflé, suit my family down to
the ground, but for a speedy, tasty, and filling lunch my
preference is for fish baked in a foil parcel. The fish, whether
a whole trout, or a fish fillet, cooks so beautifully on its own,
leaving more time for you to do what you want. The great
thing about this simple recipe is that it turns out well every
time, and the accompanying salad and boiled potatoes can be
prepared in the same length of time as the fish.

Fish is also part of my family tradition. Ever since I can remember,
pickled herrings has always been one of the dishes which my
family has in the larder from Christmas Eve onward. Cookies
taste wonderful during the festive season, but sooner or later
you need something more substantial, and a pickled herring,
or plate of herring salad, fits the bill nicely. Fish is no longer cheap,
as it was in my youth, but you should try to include it in your
weekly meal plan, because it is good for your health and
easy to digest.

Fish Soup
Fischsuppe (Fischfond)

Serves 6–8

3 pounds assorted fish heads, tails, etc. (ensure that the assortment contains a few salmon heads)
10 peppercorns, Cloves to taste, Salt to taste
4½–5 pounds assorted firm-fleshed fish, cleaned and gutted
3 carrots, peeled and grated, 4–5 ounces fresh shrimp, shelled and deveined
Freshly ground pepper to taste, Splash of dry white wine to taste
1 bunch of fresh dill, chopped

1. Rinse the bones, salmon heads, and fins under cold, running water, and drain them in a colander, then put in a large saucepan with the peppercorns, and cloves. Fill the saucepan with cold water, season with salt, and bring it to a boil. Reduce the heat and simmer the fish trimmings over a low heat for about 45 minutes.

2. Strain the resulting fish stock through a fine sieve into a clean saucepan. Discard the fish trimmings.

3. Rinse the fish under cold, running water, then divide into medium-sized portions and add them to the fish stock, together with the grated carrots, and shrimp. Simmer gently until the fish is cooked through but not disintegrating, then season to taste with salt and pepper, and add some white wine. Transfer the soup to a soup terrine and garnish it with the chopped dill.

Even my husband enjoys this soup!

French Fish Soup
(Französischer Fischtopf)

Serves 4

2 pounds assorted salt water fish, cleaned and gutted (the greater the variety, the better)
3 onions
¾ stick butter
2 bay leaves
3 peppercorns
½ teaspoon fresh thyme
Salt and freshly ground pepper to taste
2 cups white Muscatel wine
2–4 cloves of garlic, peeled and finely minced
1 French bread stick

1. Rinse the fish under cold, running water, and cut them into even-sized pieces.

2. Peel and chop the onions. Melt 3½ tablespoons of the butter in a saucepan, and sauté the onions in it until translucent. Add the fish portions, bay leaves, peppercorns, thyme, salt, and pepper. Mix all these ingredients together.

3. Pour the Muscatel wine over the fish, and dot the remaining butter on top.

4. Bring the pan to a boil, reduce the heat, put a lid on the pan, and simmer the soup over a low heat for about 30 minutes.

5. Slice the French stick and toast the slices. Spread them with the finely minced garlic, and serve with the soup.

Salt Cod and Potato Bake
(Stockfisch mit Kartoffeln)

Serves 6–8

2 pounds potatoes, boiled
¼ cup anchovies, or ½ salted herring
3½ pounds salt cod, desalted and boiled
¾ stick butter
1 tablespoon fresh breadcrumbs
4 eggs
1 cup heavy cream
Pinch of salt to taste
Freshly ground pepper to taste

1. Peel the boiled potatoes and slice them thin.

2. Bone the anchovies, or herring, and dice them fine.

3. Bone the salt cod and cut it into chunks.

4. Preheat the oven to 350°F. Grease an ovenproof dish with 4 teaspoons of the butter. Alternately layer the dried cod, sliced potato, a few pieces of anchovy, or herring, and breadcrumbs, until the ingredients are used up. Finish with a layer of breadcrumbs.

5. Beat together the eggs and cream, and season the mixture with the salt and pepper. Pour the egg mixture over the bake. Dot the top of the bake with the remaining butter. Bake for 30 minutes. Serve with a mixed salad.

Poached Trout
(Forelle in eigener Sauce)

Serves 4

4 trout, cleaned and gutted
1 scant tablespoon all-purpose flour
1 scant tablespoon fresh breadcrumbs
Salt and freshly ground pepper to taste
Freshly grated nutmeg to taste
1 onion, peeled and finely diced
1 tablespoon chopped fresh parsley
2 bay leaves
2–3 cloves
A few slices of lemon
3 tablespoons fish stock
3 tablespoons dry white wine
Splash of white wine vinegar to taste

1. Rinse the trout, pat them dry, and lay them side by side in an ovenproof dish.

2. Combine the flour, breadcrumbs, salt, pepper, and nutmeg. Sprinkle this mixture over the trout. Preheat the oven to 400°F.

3. Mix together the diced onion and chopped parsley. Scatter this mixture over the trout. Place the bay leaves, cloves, and lemon slices on top, then combine the fish stock, white wine, and white wine vinegar, and pour this mixture over the trout. Bake for 30 minutes.

This method of preparing fish is also suitable for many other varieties. I like preparing fish fillets in this way.

Trout Parcels
(Lachsforelle in der Folie)

Serves 4

4 trout, cleaned and gutted
1 bunch fresh dill
2 tablespoons butter
1 large sheet heavy-duty aluminum foil
Salt and freshly ground pepper to taste
1 lemon, sliced

1. Rinse the trout carefully, especially the gills. Finely chop half the dill. Tie the other half into four bunches.

2. Spread the butter over the foil, and season it with salt and pepper. Spread half the chopped dill over the buttered foil.

3. Preheat the oven to 400°F. Place the trout on the foil. Season the belly cavities with the salt and insert a bunch of dill into each cavity. Sprinkle the top of each trout with salt, and the remaining chopped dill. Fold the long sides of the foil in loosely over the trout. Fold the short sides inward and upward, toward the middle of the parcel, put them together, and fold them over several times, so the fish juices cannot escape. Place the fish parcels on a baking sheet, and bake for 20–25 minutes.

4. Remove the cooked trout from the foil parcel. Arrange them on a warmed serving dish, and garnish with slices of lemon.

Cooking time depends on the size of the fish. A portion of fish of about 10 ounces would certainly be cooked in 20 minutes.

Whiting in White Wine
(Felchen in Weißwein)

Serves 4

1 pound whiting fillets, skinned and boned
Salt and freshly ground pepper to taste
Splash of lemon juice to taste
Dash of Worcestershire sauce to taste
1 tablespoon all-purpose flour
8 teaspoons butter
1 cup dry white wine
2 large tomatoes, skinned, seeded and diced
1 teaspoon chopped fresh parsley
1 teaspoon chopped fresh dill
2 tablespoons heavy cream, whipped

1. Rinse the whiting fillets and pat them dry. Season the fillets with salt, pepper, lemon juice, and Worcestershire sauce. Coat them in 2 teaspoons of the flour.

2. Melt 2 tablespoons of the butter in a skillet, and seal the whiting fillets in it. Pour the white wine over the fillets and add the diced tomatoes, parsley, and dill. Poach the whiting until they are tender.

3. Take the whiting out of the skillet, arrange on a warmed serving dish, cover with foil, and keep warm.

4. Knead together the remaining flour and butter, to make a *beurre manié*. Whisk pieces of the *beurre manié* into the liquid in the skillet, until the sauce thickens. Bring the sauce to a boil and then simmer until it is thick and smooth. Gently stir in the whipped cream. Pour the sauce over the whiting. Serve with boiled potatoes, or crusty, white bread.

Sautéed Eel
(Gebratener Aal)

Serves 4

1 prepared eel
Salt and freshly ground pepper to taste
10–12 large sage leaves
8 teaspoons butter
1 lemon, cut into wedges

1. Buy the eel already skinned and cut into chunks. Wash the eel chunks, pat them dry, then rub the salt and pepper into them.

2. Wrap each piece of eel around a sage leaf and tie it up with thread.

3. Melt the butter in a skillet. Sauté the eel tournedos in the butter on both sides, over a medium heat, until golden brown.

4. Take the eel out of the pan, and arrange it on a dish, garnished with the lemon wedges. Serve with salad and crusty, white bread.

Poached Shellfish

(Gekochter Schellfisch)

Serves 4

4 cups fish stock
2 pounds shellfish of your choice

1. Prepare a Fish Stock according to the recipe on page 52. Pour the stock into a medium-sized saucepan and bring to a boil.

2. Clean and prepare the shellfish. Add the shellfish to the boiling fish stock. Reduce the heat and cook the shellfish.

3. Drain the shellfish and arrange on a warmed dish. Serve with one of the following sauces.

Sauces as accompaniments

Each serves 4

Anchovy sauce
¼ stick butter
1 tablespoon chopped anchovies

Melt the butter in a pan and soften the anchovies in it.

Mustard sauce
¼ stick butter, 1 teaspoon Dijon-style mustard
1 teaspoon mild mustard

Melt the butter in a pan and stir in the mustards.

Paprika sauce
¼ stick butter, 2 tablespoons diced onion
2 pinches sweet paprika, 1 cup sour cream

Melt the butter in a saucepan and sauté the onions until they are translucent. Add the paprika, then stir in the sour cream.

Béarnaise sauce
2 tablespoons diced shallots
1 bouquet garni (tarragon, thyme, and chervil)
2 tablespoons good quality white wine vinegar
½ cup dry white wine, 3 egg yolks
¼ stick butter, chilled and diced

1. Put the diced shallot, bouquet garni, vinegar, and wine in a saucepan, and bring it to a boil. Continue boiling until the liquid is reduced by half. Strain the reduction through a sieve, and allow it to cool.

2. Add the egg yolks to the reduction, whisking constantly, with a balloon whisk.

3. Just before serving, reheat the sauce, stirring all the time, and gradually beat in the butter. The result should be a smooth, creamy sauce.

Hollandaise sauce
6 egg yolks
3 tablespoons all-purpose flour
¼ stick butter, chilled and diced
2 cups fish stock
1 tablespoon lemon juice

Put the egg yolks in a bowl, over a pan of simmering water. Gradually add the flour, stirring all the time. Continue stirring, and add the diced butter, a piece at a time, then the fish stock, and finally the lemon juice. Continue to stir until it is thick and creamy.

Salmon Soufflé with Shrimp Sauce
(Lachspudding mit Krabbensauce)

Serves 4

For the soufflé
1½ pounds salmon, 3 eggs, separated
¾ stick butter, softened, 13 tablespoons fresh breadcrumbs
2 tablespoons diced onion, 2–3 tablespoons chopped fresh dill
Salt and freshly ground pepper to taste, Freshly grated nutmeg to taste
1–2 tablespoons heavy cream, Butter and dry breadcrumbs for the soufflé dish
For the shrimp sauce:
8 teaspoons butter, 2 tablespoons all-purpose flour
1 cup hot fish stock, 1 cup whole milk, Salt and freshly grated nutmeg to taste,
Squeeze of lemon juice to taste, 2–3 tablespoons chopped fresh dill
8 ounces fresh shrimp, shelled and deveined

1. For the soufflé: Grind the salmon in a food processor, and refrigerate it. Whisk the egg whites until stiff, and refrigerate them.

2. Preheat the oven to 350°F. Beat the egg yolks and softened butter together, until light and fluffy. Fold in the ground salmon, breadcrumbs, diced onion, and chopped dill. Season with salt, pepper, and nutmeg. Carefully fold in the egg whites. If the mixture is too stiff, fold in 1–2 tablespoons of the cream.

3. Butter a pudding basin, or soufflé dish, and dust it with the dry breadcrumbs. Transfer the soufflé mixture to the pudding basin, or soufflé dish. Stand the pudding basin in a roasting pan, and fill the pan with water so that it comes halfway up the sides of the pudding basin. Cook the soufflé for 60 minutes until risen and golden-brown on top. Check the roasting pan occasionally, to make sure the water has not evaporated. Top it up with hot water as necessary.

4. For the sauce: Melt the butter in a saucepan and add the flour, stirring all the time. Cook the flour until it starts to froth, then add the hot fish stock, stirring constantly. Add the milk and bring the sauce to a boil, stirring all the time, until the sauce has thickened.

5. Season the sauce with salt, nutmeg, and lemon juice. Finally fold in the chopped dill and the shrimp. Reduce the heat, and allow the sauce to simmer until the shrimp are cooked through.

6. Remove the cooked soufflé from the *bain-marie* and dry the base of the soufflé dish before bringing it to the table. Pour a little shrimp sauce over the soufflé. Serve the remaining sauce separately in a sauce boat.

This soufflé can be served either as a warm starter, or as a main dish.
A medium-dry or dry white wine is a superb accompaniment.

Pike Quenelles
(Hechtklößchen)

Serves 4

6 poached pike fillets, weighing
1–1¼ pounds in total
Equal weight of heavy cream to pike fillets
6 slices white bread, crusts removed
6 shallots, peeled and finely chopped
1 egg, beaten
Salt to taste
Freshly grated nutmeg to taste
Freshly ground pepper to taste
Fish stock

1. Cut the cooled pike fillets into chunks. Grind them with the bread and chopped shallots. Mix ½ cup cream and the beaten egg into the ground fish.

2. Cover the mixture and refrigerate it for 20 minutes.

3. Grind the mixture again, then force through a fine sieve. Fold in the remaining cream and season with salt, nutmeg, and pepper. Refrigerate the mixture again.

4. Put the fish stock in a saucepan, and bring it to a boil. Reduce the heat, until the stock is simmering gently. Dampen two teaspoons, and use them to shape portions of the pike mixture into little dumplings, or quenelles. Drop the quenelles into the simmering fish stock, and cook them until they float to the surface.

I like serving these quenelles on a bed of wilted, fresh spinach. Ravioli stuffed with this pike forcemeat tastes very good.

Summer Flounder with Bacon
(Sommerflunder mit Speck)

Serves 4

4 medium-sized, prepared flounder (or sole)
Salt to taste
1 tablespoon flour
4 tablespoons corn oil
4 teaspoons butter
6 slices bacon

1. Rinse the summer flounder, and pat them dry. Season them lightly on both sides with salt and dust them with the flour.

2. Heat the oil and butter in a large skillet and sauté the summer flounder in it, turning them occasionally, until they are golden brown on both sides.

3. Dice the bacon fine, and sauté in another skillet until crisp. Drain the bacon on absorbent kitchen paper, and scatter over the plaice. Serve the summer flounder with potato salad, or green asparagus.

The summer flounder tastes even better if you sauté ½ cup of slivered almonds with the diced bacon and scatter them over the fish.

Sautéed Herrings
(Bratheringe)

Serves 4

10 prepared herrings
Salt and freshly ground pepper to taste
Flour for dusting
4–6 tablespoons corn oil
1 cup white wine vinegar
Splash of water
1 onion, peeled and sliced
10 peppercorns
Oil for drizzling

1. Rinse the herrings, pat them dry, season with salt and pepper, then toss them in the flour.

2. Heat the oil in a large skillet and sauté the herrings, turning them occasionally, until they are golden brown on both sides. Remove them from the skillet and drain them on absorbent kitchen paper, then place in a deep dish.

3. Put the vinegar, a splash of water, the sliced onion, and peppercorns in a saucepan. Bring to a boil and simmer for a few minutes, to form a strong marinade.

4. Pour the hot marinade over the herrings. When the marinade has cooled, drizzle a little oil over the herrings. Allow the herrings to marinate for at least 24 hours.

Pickled Herrings
(Eingelegte Heringe)

Serves 4

10 salted herrings
2 ripe cooking apples
1 onion
1 cup heavy cream
1 cup sour cream
4 bay leaves
10 juniper berries
10 peppercorns

1. Soak the salted herrings in cold water for at least 12 hours, changing the water frequently.

2. Skin and bone the herrings, fillet them, then rinse them.

3. Peel, core, and quarter the apples. Peel and quarter the onion. Cut the apple and onion quarters into thin, diagonal slices. Mix together the heavy cream and sour cream. Add the bay leaves, juniper berries, and peppercorns to the cream.

4. Alternately layer the herring fillets, sliced apple, sliced onion, and cream in a large stone crock. Finish with a layer of the cream marinade. Cover, refrigerate, and allow to marinate for at least 24 hours.

Marinated Sardines
(Marinierte Sardinen)

Serves 4

1 pound prepared sardines
Salt to taste
Flour for dusting
½ cup olive oil
1 cup tarragon vinegar
2 bay leaves
2 cloves
1 bunch fresh thyme, chopped
1 onion, peeled and thinly sliced
2 cloves of garlic, peeled and thinly sliced

1. Wash the sardines, pat them dry, season with salt, and toss them in the flour.

2. Heat the olive oil in a skillet and sauté batches of the sardines in it, over a medium heat, until they are golden brown on both sides.

3. Drain the sardines on absorbent kitchen paper and place them in a shallow dish.

4. Put the vinegar, bay leaves, cloves, and chopped thyme in a saucepan, with the sliced onions, and garlic. Bring to a boil. Strain the hot vinegar through a sieve, pouring the liquid over the sardines.

5. Cover the sardines and leave them in the refrigerator overnight to marinate. Serve with crisp, white toast.

Prepared in this way, anchovies also taste delicious too.

Gravlax
(Gebeizter Lachs)

Serves 12

1 fresh, prepared salmon, weighing about 4½ pounds
1 bunch fresh dill
5 tablespoons salt
¼ cup white sugar
2 tablespoons coarsely ground white peppercorns

1. Cut the salmon in half lengthwise. Bone the salmon halves, and place one half of the salmon skin-side down in a deep dish. Arrange the sprigs of dill on top of the salmon. Sprinkle the salt, sugar, and pepper over it. Place the other salmon half on top, flesh side down. Cover the salmon with foil. Place a wooden chopping board on top of the salmon and weigh it down with a heavy weight.

2. Marinate the salmon for 2–3 days. Turn it every day, morning and night, and baste it with the liquor that forms. Gently open the belly cavity, so you can baste it with the marinade.

3. Pat the marinated salmon dry with kitchen paper and cut the flesh away from the skin in thin slices. Serve the sliced salmon with slices of lemon and creamed horseradish.

A juicy roast is a great pleasure. Sadly, it is becoming increasingly difficult to prepare one, because success starts with the quality of the meat. If the quality of the meat is not high enough, even the best cook, with the most stylish recipe, won't be able to produce a first class dish.

You should think yourself lucky if you are able to buy meat direct from the producer. If you live in town, as I do, then it's rather difficult. Be that as it may, find yourself a good butcher, whom you trust and who, most importantly, still knows where he gets his meat from, even if it means you have to go out of your way to shop there. In the meantime, you should take greater care than ever about where your meat comes from! Cooking meat can also be fun, and offers an incredible range of potential cooking methods. Depending on whether it is stewed, braised, roasted, pan-fried or barbecued, the taste is completely different.

We particularly enjoy recipes based on ground meat, but, take my word for it, I have never bought ready-ground meat. As long as I've been cooking for my family, I have bought a suitable cut of meat from the butcher and I either get him to grind it for me, or I do it myself, at home. This is why my recipes based on ground meat are not second-class dishes, but can hold their own with any roast joint.

Stuffed Breast of Veal

(Gefüllte Kalbsbrust)

Serves 4

2 pounds breast or loin of veal, boned, Salt to taste
2 slices of white bread, crusts removed, ½ stick butter
I small onion, peeled and finely diced, 2 cups pork sausage meat
I tablespoon chopped fresh parsley, 3 eggs, beaten
Freshly ground pepper to taste, Pinch of grated lemon zest
I carrot, peeled and finely chopped, I onion, peeled and finely chopped

1. Wash the breast, or loin, of veal, pat it dry, and season the inner pocket with salt.

2. Put the bread slices in a dish with a splash of water. Leave them to soak. Melt 4 teaspoons of the butter in a skillet, and sauté the diced onion. Add the sausage meat and the chopped parsley, and sauté them with the onion. Take the skillet off the heat. Drain the bread slices, squeeze them out, and break into pieces. Mix the pieces of softened bread into the stuffing mixture. Work the stuffing until it forms a smooth paste. Allow it to cool. Stir the beaten eggs into the stuffing and season it with salt, pepper, and grated lemon zest. Stuff the inner pocket in the veal with the stuffing mixture. Sew up the pocket with thread.

3. Preheat the oven to 400°F. Melt 2 tablespoons of the remaining butter in a roasting pan, and seal the meat in it on all sides. Briefly sweat the chopped carrot and onion with the veal. Deglaze the pan with a little water, and transfer the roasting pan to the oven. Roast the veal for about 1½ hours, basting it occasionally with the remaining butter, and the pan juices.

The breast, or loin, of veal can also be cooked in a stock consisting of 1 cup of dry white wine, 1 cup of good quality white wine vinegar, and 2 cups of water, but it won't be as tasty.

Marinated Veal Rump
(Gebeizter Kalbsschlegel)

Serves 8

4½ pounds veal rump, or silverside, boned
⅓ cup + 1½ tablespoons white wine vinegar
1¾ pints water, A few peppercorns to taste
A few crushed juniper berries to taste
1 bay leaf, 4 slices bacon
2 onions, peeled and finely chopped
1 parsley root, peeled and finely chopped
1 carrot, peeled and finely chopped
2 cloves, Freshly grated nutmeg to taste
1 cup hot veal stock
8 teaspoons melted butter
¾ cup sour cream

1. Rinse the veal rump, or silverside, remove the skin, and place it in a large dish.

2. Put the vinegar, water, peppercorns, bay leaf, and juniper berries in a saucepan and bring them to a boil. Pour the marinade over the veal. Cover and marinate for 2 days.

3. Preheat the oven to 400°F. Take the veal out of the marinade, pat it dry, and lard it with the slices of bacon. Reserve some of the marinade. Put the veal in a roasting pan with the chopped onions, parsley root, carrot, and cloves. Season with the nutmeg. Roast the veal, basting it with the hot stock, melted butter, and ½ cup of the sour cream. Turn it occasionally, and cook it until the meat is well done.

4. Transfer the veal to a serving dish. Strain the gravy through a sieve, into a clean saucepan. Blend in the remaining sour cream, and flavor it with a little of the vinegar marinade. Bring to a boil, and simmer for a few minutes so it thickens and the flavors combine.

Roast Veal in Gorgonzola Cheese
(Kalbsbraten im Gorgonzolamantel)

Serves 8

4½ pounds veal rump or silverside, boned
Salt and freshly ground pepper to taste
½ stick butter, 4 onions, peeled and diced
3½ pounds mushrooms, wiped and thinly sliced
1½ cups Gorgonzola cheese, mashed
3 cups heavy cream, 2 tablespoons cognac
2 level tablespoons all-purpose flour
1 tablespoon chopped fresh dill
1 tablespoon chopped fresh watercress

1. Preheat the oven to 400°F. Rub the veal with 4 teaspoons of butter, salt, and pepper. Roast for 1 hour, basting frequently with the pan juices. Melt the remaining butter in a skillet, and sauté the onion until translucent. Add the mushrooms, and sweat them until all the juices have evaporated. Season with salt and pepper.

2. Beat together the gorgonzola, ½ cup of the cream, and the cognac to form a paste. After the veal has been roasting for 1 hour, spread half of this paste over it. Add the onion and mushroom mixture to the roasting pan, with ½ cup of the cream. Roast the veal for a further 30 minutes. Spread the remaining cheese mixture over the veal. Increase the oven temperature to 430°F, and roast for another 30 minutes.

3. Beat 1 cup of the cream with the flour. Stir it into the pan juices. Add the remaining cream after 20 minutes. Turn the oven off and allow the veal to rest for 10 minutes. Take the meat out and slice it. Arrange the mushroom and cream mixture on a serving dish, place the sliced veal on top, and garnish it with the chopped dill and watercress.

Roast Loin of Veal
(Kalbsnierenbraten)

Serves 6–8

4½ pounds loin of veal, boned and rolled
Salt and freshly ground pepper
½ stick butter
2 tablespoons corn oil
1 onion, peeled and chopped
1 carrot, peeled and chopped

1. Preheat the oven to 400°F. Rub the loin of veal with the salt and pepper.

2. Heat the oil and 4 teaspoons of the butter in a roasting pan. Seal the veal all over in the hot oil. Add the chopped onion and carrot, and sweat them in the oil. Deglaze the pan with a little water.

3. Melt the remaining butter. Roast the meat for about 2 hours. Brush the veal with the melted butter during cooking, baste it with the pan juices, and turn it occasionally. Roast the veal until it is golden brown and tender.

4. Take the meat out of the oven and allow it to rest before carving it. Strain the pan juices through a sieve, into a clean saucepan. Bring to a boil and simmer for a few minutes to reduce and thicken.

Larded Calf's Heart
(Gespicktes Kalbsherz)

Serves 4

1–2 calf's hearts, depending on size
6 cups veal stock
3 slices bacon, cut into thin strips
Salt to taste, 1 tablespoon all-purpose flour
1 tablespoon corn oil, ½ stick butter
1 onion, peeled and finely chopped
1 carrot, peeled and finely chopped
Splash of white wine, lemon juice, or vinegar

1. Cut the calf's hearts in half, wash them thoroughly, and pat them dry. Put the veal stock in a saucepan, bring it to a boil, add the calf's hearts to the pan, and blanch them briefly in the stock.

2. Take the hearts out of the stock, and allow them to cool a little. Reserve the stock. Lard the calf's hearts with the slices of bacon. Season them with salt and toss them in the flour until well coated.

3. Heat the oil and butter in a flameproof casserole dish and sauté the hearts until they are sealed. Add the chopped onion and carrot and sweat. Add a splash of veal stock to the casserole dish to deglaze it, cover it, and braise the hearts for about 40 minutes.

4. Take the hearts out of the casserole dish, and keep them warm. Strain the pan juices through a sieve into a clean saucepan. Add a splash of wine, lemon juice, or vinegar, so that the gravy tastes slightly acidic, and bring the gravy to a boil quickly.

5. Slice the hearts, add them to the gravy, and serve with mashed or boiled potatoes.

Sautéed Calf's Head
(Gebackener Kalbskopf)

Serves 4

1 calf's head, split, 8 ounces veal
1 carrot, peeled and finely chopped
1 onion, peeled and finely chopped
2 bay leaves, A few peppercorns to taste
A few crushed juniper berries to taste
Grated zest of 1 lemon
Salt and freshly ground pepper to taste
2–3 tablespoons chopped fresh parsley
2 eggs, beaten
⅓ cup + 6½ tablespoons fresh breadcrumbs
2 tablespoons butter, 2 tablespoons corn oil

1. Wash the calf's head thoroughly. Bring a large saucepan of salted water to a boil, add the calf's head, veal, carrot, onion, bay leaves, lemon zest, peppercorns, and juniper berries. Simmer until the meat is tender.

2. Remove the calf's head and veal from the stock and allow them to cool a little. Reserve the stock. Take the meat off the calf's head. Finely chop both this meat and the piece of veal. Season the chopped meat with salt, pepper, and chopped parsley. Put the meat into a 3½ pint dish, or terrine. Press the meat down firmly and add a splash of the veal stock to help bind it. Put the dish in the refrigerator to allow the veal mixture to set overnight.

3. Cut the veal terrine into thick slices. Coat the slices in the beaten egg, then in the bread-crumbs. Melt the butter and oil in a skillet. Sauté the slices in the butter and oil mixture over a high heat, until they are golden brown on both sides. Serve with potato salad.

Ox Tongue in White Wine
(Kalbszunge in Weißwein)

Serves 4

1–2 ox tongues
Salt to taste
2 carrots, peeled and chopped
1 celeriac, peeled and chopped
1 leek, peeled and chopped
Small bunch of fresh parsley, chopped
½ stick butter
Splash of corn oil
8 teaspoons all-purpose flour
½ cup veal stock
½ cup dry white wine
3–4 tablespoons capers

1. Soak the ox tongues in cold water for an hour, then rinse them in cold, running water. Bring a large saucepan of salted water to a boil, add the tongue, chopped carrots, celeriac, leek, and parsley to the pan, and simmer until the tongue is tender.

2. Remove the cooked tongue from the stock, and allow it to cool a little. Remove the skin, and cut it in half lengthways.

3. Heat the butter and oil in a saucepan. Add the flour to the pan, stirring all the time. Continue stirring until the flour froths. Add the veal stock and dry white wine, stirring all the time, and continue cooking until the sauce thickens. Add the capers to the sauce. Put the tongue in the sauce and reheat it thoroughly.

Sauerbraten
(Sauerbraten)

Serves 6

<u>For the marinade:</u>
2 cups red wine vinegar, 4½ cups water
1 carrot, peeled and chopped, 2 onions, peeled and chopped
2 bay leaves, 4–5 peppercorns, 2 cloves, 5–7 juniper berries, crushed
<u>For the roast:</u>
2 pounds beef (top rump or sirloin), 3 tablespoons corn oil,
Crust from 1 slice rye bread, or pumpernickel, 1 onion, peeled and chopped
1 carrot, peeled and chopped, 1 parsley root, 2 tomatoes,
⅓ cup + 1½ tablespoons red wine, 2 tablespoons all-purpose flour

1. <u>For the marinade:</u> Mix together the red wine vinegar and water. Add the chopped carrot, onion, bay leaves, peppercorns, cloves, and juniper berries.

2. Rinse the beef, pat it dry, put it in a large dish, and pour over the marinade. Cover and put it in a cool place. Allow the beef to marinate for 2–3 days, turning it occasionally.

3. Take the beef out of the marinade, and drain it well. Heat the oil in a roasting pan, or flameproof casserole dish, and sauté the meat in the hot oil until sealed on all sides. Add the rye bread crust, the chopped onion, carrot, parsley root, and tomatoes to the oil and sweat them briefly. Add a generous splash of the marinade, cover the roasting pan, or casserole dish, and braise the beef, basting it occasionally with more of the marinade, until tender. Take the beef out of the roasting pan, and keep it warm.

4. Whisk together the red wine and flour. Add the mixture to the pan juices and cook over a low heat until the gravy thickens. If the gravy is too thick, add a splash of marinade.

5. Purée the gravy through a sieve. Carve the beef and arrange overlapping slices on a warm serving dish. Pour a little of the gravy over the beef. Serve the remaining gravy separately. Serve the sauerbraten with steamed potato dumplings.

Goulash
(Gulasch)

Serves 4–6

2 pounds beef (brisket or shin)
3 tablespoons corn oil
I pound shallots, peeled and finely diced
Cloves of garlic to taste, peeled
Salt to taste
Freshly ground pepper to taste
Sweet paprika to taste
Ground caraway to taste
I tablespoon red wine vinegar
½ cup hot beef stock, 1¾ pints red wine
Cayenne pepper to taste

1. Rinse the beef, pat it dry, and dice it.

2. Heat the oil in a saucepan and sauté the diced shallots until translucent.

3. Add the diced beef and sauté it with the shallots. Crush the cloves of garlic in a little salt. Add it to the beef with the pepper, some of the sweet paprika, the caraway, and vinegar. Add the hot beef stock immediately and simmer the goulash over a medium heat. Gradually add the red wine, a generous splash at a time.

4. Simmer over a low heat until the meat is tender, then season the goulash to taste with the remaining sweet paprika and cayenne pepper. Simmer the goulash for a few minutes longer, so the paprika is fully incorporated and the flavors combine.

I like using a slice of pumpernickel bread to thicken the sauce. I add it after the sweet paprika, caraway, and vinegar have been added.

Paupiettes of Beef
(Rinderrouladen)

Serves 4

4 thin slices beef fillet, or sirloin
5 slices of bacon
Salt and freshly ground pepper to taste
2–3 tablespoons mild mustard
A few gherkins, thinly sliced
3 tablespoons corn oil
I onion, peeled and finely diced
I carrot, peeled and finely diced
Hot water (or hot beef stock)

1. Rinse the slices of beef, pat dry, and spread them out side by side on a large chopping board. Cut four of the bacon slices into thin strips.

2. Season the beef slices with salt and pepper, then spread them with the mustard. Cover with the bacon and gherkins, and, starting from the narrow end, roll them up to form paupiettes. Fasten with cocktail sticks. Heat the oil in a casserole dish and sear the paupiettes.

3. Finely dice the remaining gherkins and slice of bacon. Add to the paupiettes, together with the diced carrot and onion, and sauté all the ingredients. Gradually add hot water to the casserole dish, cover, and braise the paupiettes over a low heat until tender.

4. Take the paupiettes out of the casserole dish and keep them warm. Purée the gravy through a sieve. Arrange the paupiettes on a serving dish, and pour the gravy over them.

The mustard helps to make the gravy smooth, so you don't need any other thickening agent.

Beef Patties
(Fleischpfanzel)

Serves 4

1 cup ricotta cheese or fromage blanc
1–2 tablespoons rubbed dried marjoram
Salt and freshly ground pepper to taste
3 eggs, beaten
3 cups ground steak
1 onion, peeled and finely chopped
5–6 tablespoons corn oil

1. Mix together the ricotta cheese, marjoram, salt, and pepper. Leave the mixture to stand for about 30 minutes, so the flavors can combine.

2. Gradually add the beaten eggs, ground steak, and chopped onion, and work the mixture until it forms a smooth paste.

3. Scoop out small portions of the mixture with a tablespoon, then dampen your hands and use them to shape the meat into patties.

4. Heat the oil in a large skillet. Sauté the beef patties in the oil, over a medium heat, until golden-brown on both sides.

The addition of ricotta cheese makes the beef patties particularly juicy, and nicely crisp when sautéed. I also often prepare beef patties with rolled oats. I pour a scant 2 cups of water over 13 tablespoons of the oats, and leave them to swell for a few minutes. I then gradually work 3 cups ground steak and a peeled, diced onion into the oats. Season the mixture to taste, then follow the method described above. We enjoy these beef patties accompanied by potato salad.

Bolognese Sauce
(Hackfleischsauce)

Serves 4

3 tablespoons olive oil
3 large onions, peeled and finely diced
2 cups lean ground steak
2 cups ripe tomatoes, skinned and chopped
1 small carrot, peeled and finely diced
1 small piece celeriac, peeled and finely diced
Finely chopped fresh basil to taste
Finely chopped fresh oregano and thyme to taste
Salt and freshly ground pepper to taste
1 tablespoon chopped fresh parsley

1. Heat the olive oil in a casserole dish, or large saucepan. Sauté the diced onion in the oil, until translucent. Add the ground steak in batches and sauté with the onions.

2. Add the chopped tomatoes, carrot, celeriac, basil, oregano, and thyme to the steak and onions. Simmer the meat sauce over a low heat for about 1½ hours, until a smooth sauce results.

3. Finally, season the Bolognese sauce with salt and pepper, then stir in the chopped parsley.

In winter, it is better to use quality peeled plum tomatoes from a can.

Cabbage Parcels
(Krautwickel)

Serves 4

2 small heads white cabbage, 2 slices white bread, crusts removed
1 cup milk, 8 teaspoons butter, softened
2 cups ground steak, or finely chopped cold roast beef or poultry,
or sausage meat, 2 small eggs, beaten
2 tablespoons diced onion, 2 tablespoons chopped fresh parsley
Grated zest of 1 lemon, Salt and freshly ground pepper to taste
3 tablespoons corn oil, 2–3 tablespoons pork dripping for glaze

1. Strip the best leaves from the heads of cabbage. Bring a saucepan of salted water to a boil and cook the cabbage leaves in it until they are just tender.

2. Drain the cabbage leaves, then spread them out, side by side, on a board, and cut out the thick central spine. Soak the bread in the milk.

3. Beat the softened butter until creamy. Drain the bread, squeeze it out, then break off pieces and beat them into the butter. Gradually add the ground steak, beaten eggs, diced onion, and chopped parsley.

4. Season the steak mixture with the lemon zest, salt, and pepper, then work it until a smooth paste forms. Divide the steak mixture between the cabbage leaves, and spread it over them thickly. Starting at the short side, roll up the leaves to form parcels, and tie them up with thread.

5. Preheat the oven to 350°F. Heat the oil in a flameproof casserole dish. Sauté the cabbage parcels carefully over a medium heat.

6. Transfer the casserole dish to the oven. Bake the cabbage parcels for 1 hour, brushing them frequently with pork dripping, to make them crisp. If the cabbage leaves are browning too quickly, either reduce the oven temperature, or cover the casserole dish with foil.

The cabbage parcels are lovely and shiny when basted with the pork dripping. I always make a double recipe of steak mixture. I boil the remaining cabbage leaves until tender, put them through a grinder, and work the ground cabbage into the steak mixture. I shape the steak mixture into a meatloaf, or patties, and freeze them, thus having an extra meal in hand.

Paupiettes of Pork
(Schweineröllchen)

Serves 4

8 teaspoons butter
1 large onion, peeled and finely diced
2 cups sauerkraut
About 40 Thompson seedless grapes, halved
1 pound porcini, or button mushrooms
Salt and freshly ground pepper to taste
4 large, thin pork escalopes
½ cup dry white wine or champagne

1. Melt 4 teaspoons of the butter in an oven-proof casserole dish and sauté half of the diced onion in it, until translucent. Add the sauerkraut and sweat it with the onions. Add a splash of water and the grapes, then turn the heat down low and braise the mixture until well combined.

2. Wipe the mushrooms. Cut any large ones in half, or into quarters. Melt the remaining butter in a skillet and sauté the remaining diced onion. Add the mushrooms, season them with salt and pepper, and sauté them until all the liquid has evaporated.

3. Preheat the oven to 350°F. Rinse the escalopes, pat them dry, and spread them out, side by side. Season them with salt and pepper. Divide the mushroom mixture in four and spread it over the escalopes. Roll them up, starting from the short side, and secure with cocktail sticks, then place on top of the sauerkraut. Pour the wine, or champagne, over the paupiettes, cover them, and braise in the oven for about 40 minutes.

Filet Allemand
(Filet l'allemand)

Serves 6–8

4 small pork fillets, each weighing about ½ pound
Salt and freshly ground pepper to taste
Sweet paprika to taste
8–10 slices bacon
2 large onions, peeled and diced
1¾ cups heavy cream
¾ cup sour cream

1. Remove any skin and fat from the pork fillets. Rinse them, pat them dry, and cut each fillet into 3 pieces. Season the fillets with a mixture of salt, pepper, and paprika, rub the seasonings into the pork, and leave to marinate.

2. Preheat the oven to 350°F. Chop the bacon fine. Heat a skillet and sauté the bacon until translucent.

3. Scatter the chopped bacon over the base of an ovenproof dish. Layer the marinated pork on top of the bacon, then cover the pork with the diced onion. Put the dish in the oven, and roast the pork for 15–20 minutes. The onions should be translucent.

4. Combine the two creams and pour them over the layer of onions. Braise the pork for a further 30–35 minutes.

This recipe is excellent for preparing in advance and is therefore perfect for when you have guests.

Roast pork
(Schweinebraten)

Serves 6–8

3½ pounds pork shoulder, with rind
Salt and freshly ground pepper to taste
Caraway seeds to taste
1 clove of garlic, peeled and crushed
4 teaspoons butter
1 onion, peeled and finely chopped
1 piece of celeriac, peeled and chopped
1 carrot, peeled and chopped
1 parsley root, peeled and chopped
1 small piece of leek, washed and sliced
½ bunch fresh parsley, washed and coarsely chopped
1 slice stale bread, grated
½ cup beer

1. Rub the pork shoulder with salt, pepper, caraway, and finely crushed garlic. Cover the pork and put it in the refrigerator to marinate for about 1 hour.

2. Preheat the oven to 400°F. Melt the butter in a roasting pan. Seal the pork shoulder, rind side down, in the hot butter. Add the chopped onion and a splash of hot water to deglaze the pan. Put the roasting pan in the oven and roast the pork for about 1½ hours, occasionally adding more hot water.

3. Turn the shoulder of pork, so the rind is uppermost. Score the rind in a diamond pattern, using a sharp knife. Add the chopped celeriac, carrot, parsley root, leek, chopped parsley, and grated bread. Roast the pork for another hour, occasionally basting the rind with the pan juices, and the beer. A golden-brown, crisp crust should form.

Bierschinken
(Bierschinken)

Serves 12–18

1 whole leg of pork, on the bone, weighing approx. 6½–7½ pounds
Generous quantity of salt to taste
3 cloves of garlic, peeled and finely crushed
4 tablespoons Dijon-style mustard
2 tablespoons honey
3 cups beer

1. Rinse the pork, pat it dry, and coat it thickly in the salt. Place the pork shank in brine, put it in a cool place, and leave it to marinate for about 3 weeks, turning the pork shank frequently.

2. Take the pork out of the brine, drain it, and pat it dry with a dishcloth. Rub the pork with the crushed garlic.

3. Preheat the oven to 425°F. Place the pork in a roasting pan. Put it in the oven and roast it for at least 2 hours. Combine the mustard and honey and brush the pork with the mixture during cooking. As the pork roasts, baste it frequently with the beer.

Leg of Lamb in a Mustard Crust
(Lammkeule in der Senfkruste)

Serves 8

1 leg of lamb on the bone, weighing about 4½ pounds, Fresh cloves of garlic to taste
½ jar Dijon-style mustard, 1 cup mild, home-made mustard (see recipe on page 148)
½ teaspoon freshly ground pepper, 3 tomatoes, 1 large onion

1. Remove the skin and fat from the leg of lamb, rinse it, and pat dry.

2. Peel the cloves of garlic and cut them into thin slivers. Using a sharp knife, make small slits all over the leg of lamb and insert the slivers of garlic. Blend together the mustards and the pepper, then spread the mixture thickly over the lamb. Cover and leave to marinate overnight in a cool place, or in the refrigerator.

3. Preheat the oven to 400°F. Wash and roughly chop the tomatoes. Peel and roughly chop the onion. Put the tomatoes and onion in a roasting pan with the leg of lamb, and ½ cup hot water. Roast the lamb for 2–2½ hours, basting it occasionally with more hot water, and the pan juices.

4. Take the leg of lamb out of the oven and transfer it to a warmed serving dish. Remove any sections of the mustard crust which have turned very dark. Carve the lamb.

5. Purée the pan juices through a sieve, and pour the gravy over the lamb. Serve with green beans and boiled potatoes.

You don't need to season the leg of lamb before spreading the mustard over it, as the mustard mixture provides a tasty seasoning.

Lamb Strudel
(Lammstrudel)

Serves 6–8

For the strudel dough:
½ cup lukewarm water
1 egg, beaten, Salt to taste
2 teaspoons oil, 1 cup bread flour
For the filling:
1 small onion, peeled and finely diced
1 clove of garlic, peeled and finely minced
3 cups ground lamb, 2 eggs, beaten
Salt and freshly ground pepper to taste
⅓ cup melted butter

1. For the strudel dough: Mix together the water, egg, salt, and oil. Put the flour in a bowl and make a well in the center. Pour the egg mixture into the well. Mix together using the blade of a knife, then knead the dough until it is elastic. Shape into a ball, cover, and leave it to rest.

2. For the filling: Work the onion, garlic, and beaten eggs into the lamb. Season the mixture generously with salt and pepper, and beat it until a smooth paste forms.

3. Cut the ball of dough in half. Spread a large, floured cloth over the work surface, and put each piece of dough on it. Stretch out each piece carefully with the knuckles and brush with a little of the melted butter. Continue stretching it until it is very thin. Spread the lamb mixture over each piece of dough.

4. Preheat the oven to 350°F. Using the floured cloth, roll up each strudel. Fold in the ends, and press them down firmly. Place them on a greased baking sheet with the seams underneath. Brush with the remaining butter. Bake for about 1 hour until golden brown.

Braised Lamb
(Gedämpftes Lammfleisch)

Serves 4

8 small, thin lamb steaks
Salt and freshly ground pepper to taste
8 ounces ripe tomatoes
½ stick butter
½ cup dry red wine
½ cup meat stock
1–2 teaspoons cornstarch
1 tablespoon chopped fresh parsley

1. Rinse the lamb steaks, pat them dry, and season with salt and pepper.

2. Bring a saucepan of water to a boil. Immerse the tomatoes briefly in the boiling water, drain and then refresh them in cold water. Skin, halve, seed, and chop them.

3. Melt the butter in a skillet until it foams and seal the lamb steaks quickly, on both sides, in the hot butter.

4. Add the tomatoes and sweat them briefly with the lamb. Gradually add the red wine, reserving a little, and the meat stock. Cover the pan and braise the lamb steaks until tender.

5. Take the lamb out of the pan and keep it warm. Slake the cornstarch with the reserved red wine, add it to the pan, and thicken the red wine gravy with it. Arrange the steaks on a warmed, deep serving dish and pour over the red wine gravy. Sprinkle with the chopped parsley and serve the lamb with boiled, or mashed potatoes.

Sautéed Lamb's Liver with Potato Sauce
(Gebratene Lammleber mit Kartoffelsauce)

Serves 4

For the lamb's liver:
2 cups lamb's liver
2–3 tablespoons all-purpose flour
2 tablespoons clarified butter
1 tablespoon corn oil
For the potato sauce:
1 large, floury potato
8 teaspoons butter
1 cup lamb stock
1 tablespoon chopped fresh parsley
Salt and freshly grated nutmeg to taste
1–2 tablespoons white wine vinegar

1. For the lamb's liver: Remove any skin from the liver, and slice it thin. Toss the strips of liver in the flour.

2. Heat the clarified butter and oil in a skillet and sauté the strips of liver over a medium heat until just pink.

3. For the potato sauce: Peel the potato and grate it fine. Melt the butter in a saucepan and sauté the grated potato. Gradually add the lamb stock. Turn up the heat and cook the potato sauce until the potato is broken down, and a smooth sauce forms.

4. Add the parsley to the sauce and season it with salt, nutmeg, and vinegar. If the sauce is too thick, dilute with a splash more stock.

5. Just before serving, season the lamb's liver with salt.

Liver and Kidney Kebabs
(Spießchen von Leber und Niere)

Serves 4

2 calf's kidneys
½ cup of milk
10 ounces calf's liver
3 medium-sized onions, peeled
and cut into wedges
8 slices bacon, each cut into pieces
3 tablespoons corn oil
Salt and freshly ground pepper to taste
Cayenne pepper to taste

1. Remove any fat from the calf's kidneys. Steep in milk for 2 hours. Rinse them in cold water, pat dry, and cut them into pieces. Remove the white membrane; using sharp scissors is the easiest way.

2. Rinse the calf's liver, pat it dry, and cut into pieces, similar in size to the kidney pieces.

3. Spear pieces of kidney, onion, liver, and bacon alternately on metal skewers. Heat the oil in a skillet and sauté the kebabs in the hot oil, until the kidneys and liver are just pink. Season the kebabs with salt, pepper, and cayenne. Serve with boiled rice and a green mixed salad.

Roast Hare with Creamed Porcini
(Gebratener Hase mit Steinpilzen)

Serves 4

<u>For the roast hare:</u>
1 saddle of hare, 2 hare thighs, Splash of vinegar
4 slices bacon, Salt and freshly ground pepper
1 cup game or meat stock, ½ stick butter, melted
6 tablespoons sour cream
<u>For the creamed porcini:</u>
2 cups porcini mushrooms, 1 small onion
8 teaspoons butter, 1 tablespoon all-purpose flour
3–4 tablespoons meat stock, 2 tablespoons heavy cream
6 tablespoons dry red wine, Salt and freshly ground pepper
1 tablespoon chopped fresh parsley

1. <u>For the roast hare:</u> Remove the skin from the saddle and the thighs with a sharp knife. Rinse the hare portions and rub them with a cloth soaked in the vinegar. Cut the bacon into thin strips. Make slits in the hare portions with a sharp knife and insert the pieces of bacon. Rub salt and pepper into the hare portions.

2. Preheat the oven to 400°F. Place the hare portions in a large roasting pan, pour over the meat stock, and roast them for about 1 hour. During cooking, brush the hare portions with the melted butter and sour cream.

3. <u>For the creamed porcini:</u> Meanwhile carefully wipe the porcini and slice them. Peel and chop the onion. Melt the butter in a skillet until it foams, add the onions and sauté until translucent. Add the porcini and sweat them in the butter for 5–6 minutes. Sprinkle the flour over the onion and porcini mixture and add a splash of stock. Simmer the mixture until the flour has combined, and the sauce has thickened. Add the cream and simmer the sauce until it has reduced a little. Season the sauce with the red wine, salt, and pepper, and stir in the chopped parsley.

4. Take the hare portions out of the roasting pan, and leave them to rest for a few minutes. Strain the gravy through a sieve into a clean saucepan, bring it to a boil, then simmer for a few minutes, to reduce it. Take the meat off the hare portions and slice it. Arrange the sliced hare on a warmed serving dish and surround it with a ring of creamed porcini. Serve the gravy separately.

Our favorite accompaniment to this dish is Semolina Dumplings.
The recipe is on page 109.

Roast Venison
(Rehbraten)

Serves 6–8

3½ pounds haunch of venison, on the bone
and well hung
Salt and freshly ground pepper to taste
8 teaspoons clarified butter
1 carrot, peeled and sliced
2 bay leaves
A few juniper berries to taste
1 cup hot meat stock
1 cup sour cream or heavy cream
2–3 tablespoons cranberries (see recipe
on page 152)
1 tablespoon all-purpose flour
1 teaspoon butter
½ cup red wine

1. Carefully remove the skin from the haunch
of venison with a sharp knife and remove any
sinews.

2. Preheat the oven to 400°F. Rub the salt and
pepper into the venison. Melt the clarified
butter in a roasting pan and quickly seal the
venison all over.

3. Add the sliced carrot, bay leaves, and
juniper berries, and deglaze the pan with the
meat stock. Roast the venison for 2 hours,
basting it occasionally with the pan juices and
the sour cream.

4. After the venison has been roasting for an
hour, add the cranberries. Knead together the
flour and butter, to form a *beurre manié*, and
refrigerate it.

5. Take the roast venison out of the pan, and
keep it warm. Purée the gravy through a sieve
into a clean saucepan. Add the red wine, bring
the gravy to a boil, and gradually whisk pieces
of the *beurre manié* into the gravy, whisking
all the time, until the gravy thickens. Simmer
the gravy for a few minutes, then season it
generously with salt and pepper.

6. Slice the venison and arrange the slices on
a warmed serving dish. Pour a little of the
gravy over the meat. Serve the roast venison
with spätzle, mushrooms, and cranberries.

*I also prepare saddle of venison in the same
way. The only difference is that the joint takes
less time to cook.*

Chicken, turkey, pheasant, goose, and duck all play a major role in my menus. As with red meat, quality is everything. This is why, whenever I have the chance, I go to the producer – the farm. I buy either a meaty cockerel, or a freshly slaughtered duck, and of course I order my Christmas goose in good time for the festive season.

When our children were still young, I usually prepared whole birds, stuffed with flavored breadcrumbs, so that meat and accompaniment were prepared in one step. Served with a fresh, crisp salad, the result was a lovely main meal. I'm a great believer in anything that cuts down on hard work. Now that I mainly cook for my husband and myself, I tend to use the wide range of poultry portions that are available. Chicken breast portions, chicken drumsticks, or turkey escalopes can be prepared quickly and, when seasoned with herbs, or spices, can offer plenty of variety when cooking for two. We do love eating breast of goose, served on a bed of sauerkraut cooked in champagne, but I sometimes find it difficult to obtain the goose breast. In Alsace you will find freshly boned goose breasts on sale in any street market.

Stuffed Roast Chicken
(Gefülltes Brathähnchen)

Serves 4

1 whole chicken, weighing about 3½ pounds, 2–3 slices of bread, crusts removed
½ cup hot milk, Giblets from the chicken
2 small eggs, beaten, Chopped fresh rosemary to taste
1 tablespoon finely chopped fresh dill, Salt and freshly ground pepper to taste
Sweet paprika to taste, ¼ stick butter, melted
1 cup chicken stock

1. Remove the bag of giblets from the chicken. Rinse the chicken thoroughly inside and out and pat it dry.

2. Preheat the oven to 400°F. Put the bread slices in a dish and pour over the milk. Leave to soak for just a few seconds, then squeeze them out and drain off the milk. Chop the chicken giblets fine and add them to the bread with the beaten eggs, rosemary, and dill. Stir the mixture until a smooth stuffing forms, then season it with salt, pepper, and paprika.

3. Rub the chicken skin with salt, pepper, and paprika. Stuff the chicken with the bread mixture. Sew up the cavity with thread. Grease a roasting pan with butter and put the chicken in the pan.

4. Roast the chicken for 1 hour, until it is golden brown and crisp. During roasting brush the chicken with the melted butter and baste it with the chicken stock.

5. Carve the chicken. Purée the gravy through a sieve and serve separately from the chicken.

Because of the stuffing, you don't really need another accompaniment to the roast chicken, except maybe a green salad. If you have some stuffing left over you can always shape it into small balls, and roast them with the chicken for the final 15 minutes of cooking.

Chicken Breasts en Papillote
(Hähnchenbrust in der Folie)

Serves 2

2 meaty chicken breasts
Salt and freshly ground pepper to taste
2 tablespoons olive oil
Fresh sprigs of rosemary to taste

1. Rinse the chicken breasts and pat dry. Season them with salt and pepper.

2. Preheat the oven to 400°F. Take a sheet of strong foil, large enough to completely envelop the chicken breasts. Brush the foil with the oil and scatter a few rosemary needles over it.

3. Put the chicken breasts on the foil and scatter more rosemary over them. Fold the foil in over the chicken breasts and crimp the edges tightly, then place the parcel on a baking sheet. Bake the chicken breasts for 20–30 minutes.

4. Open the foil parcel. Arrange the chicken breasts on warmed plates. Pour the cooking juices from the foil over them. Serve the chicken breasts with mashed potato, or rice, and a mixed salad.

You can flavor the chicken breasts with other herbs of your choice, such as thyme, parsley, basil, or fresh cilantro leaves.

Fried Chicken Drumsticks
(Gebratene Hähnchenkeulen)

Serves 2–3

5–6 chicken drumsticks, or thighs
½ cup olive oil
Salt and freshly ground pepper to taste
Paprika to taste
1 tablespoon chopped fresh thyme
1 tablespoon chopped fresh chervil
1 teaspoon rosemary, chopped
2 eggs, beaten
½ cup fresh breadcrumbs
3 tablespoons corn oil
4 teaspoons butter

1. Remove any fat from the chicken drumsticks, rinse them, and pat dry.

2. Mix the olive oil, salt, pepper, paprika, thyme, chervil, and rosemary together, to form a marinade, and brush it thickly over the drumsticks. Put them in the refrigerator for a few hours, or preferably overnight, to marinate.

3. Take the drumsticks out of the refrigerator and drain them well. Coat them in the beaten egg, then in the breadcrumbs, pressing the breadcrumbs down well onto the drumsticks. Heat the oil and butter in a skillet, and fry the drumsticks in it over a medium heat, until crisp and golden brown. Serve the drumsticks with a choice of salads and crusty white bread.

The marinated drumsticks are also excellent for broiling, or barbecuing. They taste especially nice if you coat them in sesame seeds, instead of breadcrumbs.

Chicken on a Bed of Vegetables
(Hähnchen im Gemüsebett)

Serves 4

I whole chicken, weighing about 2½ pounds
Salt and freshly ground pepper
8 teaspoons all-purpose flour
4 teaspoons clarified butter
I½ tablespoons butter
I cup hot chicken stock
I tablespoon lemon juice
6 tablespoons dry white wine
I head of cauliflower florets, blanched
I pound blanched asparagus
I cup button mushrooms, tossed in melted butter
6–8 cherry tomatoes, skinned

1. Divide the chicken into 4 portions, season with salt and pepper, and toss in 4 teaspoons of the flour. Melt the clarified butter in a skillet and sauté the chicken portions until golden brown. Take them out of the pan and keep them warm.

2. Add the remaining flour and the butter to the pan and cook until the flour froths, stirring all the time. Add the chicken stock until the gravy thickens. Add the lemon juice and white wine.

3. Preheat the oven to 350°F. Pour the gravy into a lidded, ovenproof dish. Arrange the chicken portions on top, skin side uppermost, and surround them with the blanched vegetables. Cover the dish and bake the chicken on the middle shelf of the oven for 30 minutes. Remove the lid from the dish 10 minutes before the end of cooking. Serve the chicken with crusty white bread, or rice.

Chicken on a Bed of Potatoes
(Hähnchen im Kartoffelbett)

Serves 4

I whole chicken, weighing about 2½ pounds
Salt and freshly ground pepper to taste
I tablespoon finely chopped rosemary
I–2 tablespoons corn oil, or clarified butter
4 leeks, I pound potatoes
½ cup hot chicken stock
½ cup dry white wine

1. Cut the chicken into 4 portions. Wash them, pat dry, and then rub them all over with salt, pepper, and rosemary.

2. Heat the oil in a large skillet and sauté the chicken portions until golden brown. Take the chicken out of the skillet and keep it warm.

3. Cut the leeks in half lengthways, wash them thoroughly, and chop into 2–2½ inch pieces.

4. Peel the potatoes and slice them thick. Sauté the leeks and potatoes in the skillet juices.

5. Pour the stock and dry white wine over the vegetables. Place the chicken portions, skin side uppermost, on top of the bed of leeks and potatoes. Cover the skillet, and simmer the meat and vegetables for about 45 minutes. Serve the chicken and vegetables with crusty white bread.

If you cook these recipes in attractive, ovenproof dishes, you can serve them straight from the oven.

Chicken Fricassée
(Hühnerfrikassee)

Serves 4

1 whole chicken, weighing about 3 pounds
1 large carrot, peeled and finely chopped
1 large onion, peeled
4–5 peppercorns, 2 cloves
½ stick butter
8 teaspoons flour
Salt to taste
Freshly ground white pepper to taste
½ pound asparagus
½ pound baby button mushrooms
3–4 tablespoons dry white wine
1–2 tablespoons capers, to taste
2 egg yolks
1 tablespoon chopped fresh parsley

1. Rinse the chicken and pat it dry. Cook the chicken according to the method for Chicken Consommé on page 37.

2. Remove the chicken and reserve the stock. Skim the fat off the stock. Melt 8 teaspoons of butter and when it is foaming, add the flour, stirring all the time. When the flour has colored slightly add enough skimmed chicken stock, stirring all the time, to make a thick sauce. Season with salt and pepper.

3. Skin the chicken, bone it, and chop the meat into medium-sized chunks.

4. Peel the asparagus. Bring a saucepan of salted water to a boil and blanch the asparagus briefly. Wipe the mushrooms, cut them into quarters, and sauté them briefly in the remaining butter. Cut the asparagus into one inch pieces and add

them to the chicken sauce, with the mushrooms and chopped chicken meat.

5. Flavor the sauce with the white wine and capers, then simmer it over a low heat for a few minutes so the flavors can combine.

6. Add a splash of warm chicken stock to the egg yolks and beat them together. Fold the beaten egg yolks into the chicken sauce. Re-heat the sauce, if necessary, but do not let it boil. Sprinkle the chopped parsley over the chicken fricassée and serve with boiled potatoes, noodles, or rice.

The chicken fricassée will be especially tasty if chicken breast portions are poached in chicken stock. You need one breast portion, weighing about 5 ounces, per person. If fresh asparagus isn't in season, you can always use deep frozen, or canned asparagus.

Chicken Drumsticks in a Yogurt Coating

(Hähnchenkeulen im Joghurtmantel)

Serves 2–3

5–6 chicken drumsticks, or thighs
2 cups plain yogurt
2 tablespoons mild curry powder
2 tablespoons ground cumin
Juice of 1 lemon
Salt and freshly ground pepper to taste

1. Rinse the chicken drumsticks and pat them dry. Blend together the yogurt, curry powder, cumin, lemon juice, salt, and pepper, in a large bowl.

2. Toss the drumsticks in the yogurt mixture several times. They must be thickly coated all over in the yogurt marinade.

3. Place the drumsticks side by side in a large, ovenproof dish and pour the remaining yogurt mixture over them. Cover the dish, refrigerate it, and leave to marinate for at least 24 hours.

4. Preheat the oven to 400°F. Put the dish with the chicken drumsticks and marinade on the middle oven shelf and bake for about 40 minutes.

5. Take the drumsticks out of the dish and arrange them on a serving dish. Stir the sauce, and pour it over the drumsticks. Serve with a crusty French stick and a green salad.

You must use full fat yogurt for the marinade, because low fat yogurt curdles easily and then the sauce looks unattractive.

Sautéed Turkey Escalopes with Asparagus

(Gebratene Putenschnitzel mit Spargel)

Serves 4

1 pound white asparagus, Pinch of sugar
4 teaspoons butter, 4 turkey escalopes
Salt and freshly ground pepper to taste
1 tablespoon all-purpose flour
3 tablespoons corn oil
Asparagus water for deglazing, 1 egg yolk

1. Bring a large saucepan of salted water to a boil. Add a pinch of sugar and 2 teaspoons of the butter. Peel the asparagus, add it to the water, and cook for 15–20 minutes.

2. Rinse the escalopes, and pat them dry. Season with salt and pepper, and toss them in the flour. Shake off any excess flour.

3. Heat the oil and remaining butter in a skillet and sauté the escalopes until golden brown. Add a splash of cooking liquid from the asparagus and continue cooking the escalopes until they are tender.

4. Chop the asparagus spears into one-inch pieces. After the turkey escalopes have been cooking for about 15 minutes, add the asparagus, and warm it through.

5. Beat together the egg yolk and a splash of asparagus liquor. Add the beaten egg to the juices in the skillet to thicken them.

When asparagus is in season, I always freeze several portions and use them either for this recipe, or for the Chicken Fricassée on page 85.

Stir-fried Turkey with Seasonal Vegetables

(Putenschnitzel mit Gemüse der Saison)

Serves 4

4 turkey escalopes
3–4 tablespoons soy sauce
2 red bell peppers, 1 yellow bell pepper
2 small zucchini
½ pound sugar snap peas, 1 onion
4 tablespoons corn oil
⅓ cup + 1½ tablespoons hot chicken stock
4–5 tablespoons dry white wine
Salt and freshly ground pepper to taste

1. Rinse the turkey escalopes, pat them dry, and cut into strips. Put in a bowl and coat with the soy sauce. Leave them to marinate for at least 1 hour.

2. Halve, core, and seed the peppers. Wash the zucchini. Cut the peppers and zucchini into thin strips. Break the ends off the sugar snap peas. Peel the onion, and slice it.

3. Heat 2 tablespoons of oil in a deep skillet or wok, and quickly sauté the strips of turkey in it. Take the strips out and reserve them. Add the remaining oil to the skillet, gradually add the sliced vegetables and sauté them, stirring all the time, until they are just starting to soften.

4. Return the turkey strips to the skillet, deglaze the pan with the chicken stock and dry white wine, and bring it to a boil. Simmer the turkey for a few minutes, so the flavors can combine. Season generously with salt and pepper. Serve the turkey strips with rice, or white bread.

Pan-fried Turkey on Braised Tomatoes

(Putenschnitzel auf gedünsteten Tomaten)

Serves 4

4 turkey escalopes
Salt and freshly ground pepper to taste
1 tablespoon all-purpose flour
1 pound ripe tomatoes
1 onion
3 tablespoons olive oil
⅓ cup + 1½ tablespoons sour cream

1. Rinse the turkey escalopes, pat them dry, and cut them into thin strips. Season with salt and pepper, and coat them in the flour.

2. Bring a saucepan of water to a boil and blanch the tomatoes briefly. Skin, seed, then dice the tomatoes. Peel and dice the onion.

3. Heat the oil in a skillet, add the turkey strips, and seal them in the hot oil. Take the strips out and keep them warm. Sauté the diced onion in the skillet until translucent. Add the diced tomatoes and sweat them briefly with the onions. Fold in the turkey strips and sour cream. Cover the skillet and simmer the turkey for about 20 minutes. Serve the pan-fried turkey with rice, or crusty white bread.

Stuffed Turkey Breast
(Gefüllte Putenbrust)

Serves 8

2½ pounds turkey breast, Salt and freshly ground pepper to taste
1 medium-sized onion, peeled and diced, 2 carrots, peeled and grated
¾ cup button or oyster mushrooms, sliced, 1 bunch of fresh parsley, finely chopped
1 egg yolk, Grated zest of 1 lemon
5–6 thin slices bacon, ¾ stick butter
2 cups dry white wine, warmed, ½ cup heavy cream

1. Wash the turkey breast, pat it dry and, using a sharp knife, cut a deep pocket in it. Season the turkey breast all over, including inside the pocket, with salt and pepper.

2. Mix together the diced onion, grated carrots, sliced mushrooms, and chopped parsley. Add the egg yolk and bind all the ingredients together. Season the stuffing with lemon zest, salt, and pepper. Stuff the pocket in the turkey breast with the mixture and sew it up with thread.

3. Lard the turkey breast with the slices of bacon and tie them onto the breast with thread.

4. Preheat the oven to 430°F. Melt ½ stick of butter in a roasting pan and seal the turkey breast all over. Put the roasting pan on the middle oven shelf and roast the turkey breast for 10 minutes. Reduce the oven heat to 400°F, and roast the turkey breast for a further 50 minutes. During cooking, brush the turkey breast with the remaining butter and baste it with the warm wine.

5. Take the turkey breast out of the roasting pan and keep it warm. Stir the cream into the pan juices, bring them to a boil, then purée them through a sieve. Slice the turkey breast. Serve the turkey slices, and pass round the gravy separately.

My favorite accompaniment to this dish is plain, boiled rice!

Stuffed Roast Turkey
(Gefüllter Truthahn)

Serves 10–12

1 young oven-ready turkey, with giblets, weighing about 8 pounds
Salt and freshly ground pepper to taste
<u>Stuffing suggestion I:</u>
Turkey liver and heart, ½–¾ stick butter, softened
2 eggs, beaten, 1 bunch of fresh parsley, chopped
1 large onion, peeled and finely diced, ⅓ cup fresh breadcrumbs
Salt and freshly ground pepper to taste
<u>Stuffing suggestion II:</u>
2 pounds chestnuts, ½–¾ stick butter, 1 tablespoon sugar, 1 cup hot chicken stock
Salt and freshly ground pepper to taste, ⅓ cup melted butter for roasting

1. Rinse the turkey well, and pat it dry. Season it with salt and pepper.

<u>To make stuffing I:</u> Slice the turkey liver thinly and dice the heart. Beat the softened butter until light and fluffy. Gradually beat the sliced liver, diced heart, beaten eggs, chopped parsley, and diced onion into the butter. Gradually add enough of the breadcrumbs to make a smooth stuffing. Season the stuffing with salt and pepper.

<u>To make stuffing II:</u> Score a cross in the top of each chestnut. Put the chestnuts in a hot oven, and bake them until the skins peel back. Remove the chestnuts from the oven, allow them to cool a little, then peel them, and allow to cool completely. Put the butter and sugar in a saucepan and melt over a medium heat, stirring all the time, until they caramelize and turn a light golden color. Deglaze the pan with the stock, add the chestnuts, and simmer until the chestnuts are soft, but not crumbling. Season the chestnut mixture with salt and pepper.

2. Preheat the oven to 450°F.

3. Stuff the turkey with the filling of your choice and sew up the cavity with thread. Place the turkey in a large roasting pan and brush it with half of the melted butter. Put the turkey in the oven, roast it for 30 minutes, then reduce the heat to 325°F, and roast it for a further 2–2½ hours. During cooking, brush the turkey with the melted butter and baste it with the pan juices.

4. Remove the turkey from the oven and leave it to rest for a few minutes, then carve it into slices. Bring the gravy to a boil, simmer briefly, then strain and serve it separately. Serve the roast turkey and stuffing with mashed potato.

Stuffed Roast Duck
(Gefüllte Bauernente)

Serves 6

1 whole duck (with giblets) of 5½ pounds
Salt and freshly ground pepper to taste
2 slices stale white bread, ¾ cup hot milk
8 teaspoons butter, softened
2 eggs, beaten
Giblets from the duck, finely chopped
1 tablespoon chopped fresh parsley
1 tablespoon diced onion
Grated zest of 1 lemon
Freshly grated nutmeg to taste

1. Rinse the duck, pat dry, and rub it all over with salt and pepper.

2. Preheat the oven to 350°F. Put the bread slices in a dish and pour over the hot milk. Drain the milk from the bread and squeeze it out. Beat the butter until it is light and fluffy and gradually incorporate the beaten eggs, pieces of the softened bread, the chopped giblets, chopped parsley, and diced onion. Season the mixture with the lemon zest, nutmeg, salt, and pepper.

3. Stuff the duck with the mixture and sew up the cavity with thread. Put the duck in a roasting pan and roast it for 1½–2 hours, basting occasionally with hot water.

4. Take the duck from the pan and allow it to rest for a few minutes. Skim the fat off the gravy. Slice the duck off the bone and serve the gravy separately.

Stuffed Roast Goose
(Gefüllte Bauerngans)

Serves 8–10

1 whole goose, weighing 9 pounds
Salt and freshly ground pepper to taste
1 pound chestnuts, ½ cup chicken stock
Pinch of sugar to taste
5–6 slices of white bread, 2 cups hot milk
1 bunch fresh parsley, chopped
1 large onion, peeled and diced
Grated zest of 1 lemon
1 teaspoon chopped fresh thyme
1 large apple, finely grated, 2 eggs, beaten

1. Rub the goose all over with salt and pepper. Score a cross on each chestnut. Put them on a baking sheet in a very hot oven and roast them until the skins peel back. Remove from the oven, let them cool a little, and peel them. Put the chicken stock in a saucepan and bring it to a boil. Add the sugar and the chestnuts, then cook until the chestnuts are soft, but not crumbly. Drain thoroughly.

2. Put the bread in a dish, pour over the milk and stir until a paste forms. Fold in the parsley, onion, lemon zest, thyme, apple, and beaten eggs. Mix well, then fold in the drained chestnuts.

3. Preheat the oven to 425°F. Stuff the goose cavity and sew it up with thread. Prick the goose skin all over. Place the goose, breast uppermost, in a large roasting pan, and add a splash of water. Cover roast for 1 hour. Uncover the goose and roast for another hour, basting it occasionally with hot water. After 2 hours turn the goose, reduce the heat to 400°F, and roast for a further hour. Remove the goose from the roasting pan and carve it. Skim the fat off the gravy.

Roast Goose

(Gebratene Bauerngans)

Serves 8–10

1 whole goose, weighing 9 pounds
Salt and freshly ground pepper
2 onions, peeled
1 sprig of fresh thyme

1. Remove any fat from the goose, rinse it thoroughly, inside and out, then pat dry and prick the skin all over. Rub the goose all over with salt and pepper. Refrigerate it overnight.

2. Preheat the oven to 425°F. Put the peeled, whole onions and thyme in the goose cavity. Put the goose in a roasting pan, breast side up, and add a splash of water to the pan. Cover the goose and roast it for 1 hour.

3. Uncover the goose and roast for a further hour, basting occasionally with hot water.

4. After 2 hours' roasting time, turn the goose, reduce the heat to 400°F and let the goose brown and the skin crisp. Skim the fat off the pan juices with a spoon and add a splash more water to the pan, if necessary.

5. Roast the goose for a further hour. Carve the goose, and serve it with potato dumplings, sauerkraut, and celeriac salad.

This is the traditional way I prepare my Christmas goose, every year.

Goose or Duck Giblets

(Gans- oder Entenjung)

Serves 4

Wine vinegar, Water
1 onion, peeled and quartered
1 carrot, peeled and quartered
Grated zest of 1 lemon
Salt and freshly ground pepper
2 cloves, 2 bay leaves
Neck, wings, and giblets from the duck
3 tablespoons goose fat
2 tablespoons all-purpose flour
Pinch of sugar to taste

1. Make a marinade consisting of equal parts vinegar and water, the onion, carrot, lemon zest, salt, pepper, cloves, and bay leaves. Add the giblets, except the liver. There should be enough liquid to cover the giblets completely. Marinate the giblets for 1–2 days.

2. When you are ready to prepare the giblets, transfer the marinade and giblets to a saucepan and bring them to a boil. Simmer over a low heat until soft. A few minutes before the giblets are completely cooked, add the liver. Take the giblets out and keep them warm. Strain the stock through a sieve.

3. Melt the goose fat in a saucepan. Add the flour and sugar, and cook together, until they caramelize. Add enough stock, stirring continuously, to make a thick, smooth gravy, and simmer it until well thickened.

4. Take the meat off the bones. Dice the meat and giblets. Add the diced meat to the gravy, and reheat it. Season the gravy to taste with salt, pepper, and a splash of vinegar.

Pheasant on Champagne Sauerkraut
(Fasan auf Champagnerkraut)

Serves 4

For the roast pheasant:
2 young pheasants, weighing 1½–2 pounds each, Salt and freshly ground pepper to taste
Thin slices of bacon, 8 teaspoons melted butter

For the champagne sauerkraut:
1 medium-sized onion, 1 tablespoon pork dripping
2 pounds sauerkraut (canned or home-made)
3–4 juniper berries, crushed
1 cup Thompson seedless grapes, halved
1 cup champagne or dry sparkling wine
1 lemon, sliced

1. For the roast pheasant: Rinse the pheasants, pat them dry, season the cavities with salt and pepper, and rub the skin with salt only. Wrap the bacon slices around the pheasants and tie them onto the birds with thread.

2. Preheat the oven to 400°F. Brush a roasting pan with 4 teaspoons of the butter. Put the pheasants in the roasting pan, breast down. Roast for 30 minutes, then turn them. Roast the pheasants for a further 30–40 minutes, basting them frequently with the remaining butter and pan juices.

3. For the champagne sauerkraut: Peel and dice the onion. Melt the pork dripping in a saucepan, and sauté the onion until trans-lucent. Add the sauerkraut, the crushed juniper berries, and the halved grapes, mix well, and add a splash of water. There should be very little liquid in the saucepan. Cook the sauerkraut mixture on a low heat. Just before serving, add the champagne.

4. Take the pheasants out of the roasting pan and remove the slices of bacon. Carve the birds and arrange slices of breast meat on a bed of champagne sauerkraut. Garnish with slices of lemon and serve with fluffy mashed potato.

Crispy breast of goose is also wonderfully tasty when served on a bed of champagne sauerkraut.

Partridge in Madeira
(Rebhühner in Madeirasauce)

Serves 2

2 whole partridges
1 black truffle, slivered, ½ stick butter
2 shallots, peeled and finely diced
1 carrot, peeled and finely diced
1 piece of celeriac, finely diced
1 leek, finely chopped
1 bunch parsley, finely chopped
1–1½ tablespoons all-purpose flour
1 cup hot chicken stock
Salt and freshly ground pepper to taste
1½ cups Madeira wine
2 tablespoons lemon juice
4 teaspoons clarified butter

1. Bone the breasts from both partridges, and spike them with the slivered black truffle.

2. Chop the rest of the partridges into small portions. Melt 4 teaspoons of butter in a saucepan and sauté the partridge portions, together with the shallots, carrot, celeriac, leek, and parsley. Sprinkle the flour over the meat and vegetables, and stir until it is well combined. Add the hot stock, stirring all the time, and season with salt and pepper. Bring to a boil, simmer for a few minutes, then strain the meat and vegetables through a sieve. Reserve the stock. Take the meat off the bones.

3. Melt the remaining butter, and sauté the seasoned partridge breasts in it for 10 minutes. Deglaze the pan with the reserved partridge stock and cook for a further 15 minutes. Flavor the gravy with the Madeira and lemon juice. Serve on toasted white bread.

Stuffed Roast Pigeon
(Gefüllte gebratene Tauben)

Serves 4

4 whole pigeons
Salt and freshly ground pepper to taste
<u>For the stuffing:</u>
½ stick butter
1 egg, ¼ cup fresh breadcrumbs
Giblets from the pigeons, finely chopped
2 tablespoons diced onion
1 tablespoon chopped fresh parsley
Grated zest of 1 lemon
⅓ cup melted butter

1. Rinse the pigeons inside and out, pat them dry, and season with salt and pepper.

2. <u>For the stuffing:</u> Beat the butter until it is light and fluffy. Add the egg, breadcrumbs, giblets, diced onion, and chopped parsley. Season the stuffing generously with the lemon zest, salt, and pepper, and work it until the mixture forms a smooth paste.

3. Preheat the oven to 400°F. Stuff the pigeons and fasten the cavities with a toothpick. Brush a roasting pan with 4 teaspoons of butter and place the pigeons in it. Roast the pigeons for 45 minutes, basting them with the remaining butter and the pan juices.

4. Take the pigeons out of the roasting tin and cut each of them in half. Strain the gravy. Serve the pigeons with bread pudding and the gravy.

When I was a child, this was my birthday dinner.

*T*he days when big pieces of meat were a status symbol
are long gone. The influence of foreign cuisines, and not least
awareness of our own traditions, have contributed to a change
in eating habits, particularly amongst younger people.
If you go back one or two generations, eating meat during
the week was not particularly common, which meant that the
Sunday roast was even more welcome.

This chapter is a very strong reminder of my Bavarian home.
I have picked up many of these recipes at various stages
in my own life. Lower Bavarian, Franconian, and Swabian
cookery provide an incredible choice of hearty flour-based
dishes to tempt the tastebuds of any gourmet – rye spätzle with
sauerkraut salad, bread pudding with porcini, or the many spicy
potato dishes. You don't notice the lack of meat, although many
of these dishes can also be served as an accompaniment to
meat or fish, as you choose.

Homemade Pasta Ribbons with Gorgonzola Sauce

(Selbstgemachte Nudeln mit Gorgonzolasauce)

Serves 4

For the pasta ribbons:
13 tablespoons all-purpose flour, 2 eggs, ½ teaspoon salt, Splash of water
For the gorgonzola sauce:
2 cups heavy cream, 13 tablespoons crème fraîche
About ½ pound gorgonzola cheese, cubed, 3 tablespoons dry white wine
Freshly grated nutmeg to taste, Salt to taste, ¼ cup walnuts, roughly chopped

1. For the pasta ribbons: Sift the flour onto a pastry board or work surface. Make a well in the center. Break the eggs into the well and add the salt. Using a fork, gradually mix a little of the flour into the eggs.

2. Using your hands, knead the flour and eggs to form a smooth dough. If the dough is too dry, add a splash of water, and quickly knead it into the dough. Continue kneading until the surface is silky-smooth.

3. Cover the dough and allow it to rest, at room temperature, for at least 30 minutes.

4. Roll out the dough into thin sheets, either on a floured pastry board or work surface, using a noodle rolling pin, or a pasta machine.

5. Dust the pasta sheets with a pinch of flour, lay them out side by side, and allow them to dry a little.

6. Using a sharp knife, cut the dough into ribbons, or use the appropriate attachment on the pasta machine.

7. Lightly dust the pasta ribbons with a pinch of flour, so they do not stick together, and allow them to dry.

8. Bring a large pan of salted water to a boil.

9. For the gorgonzola sauce: Combine the heavy cream and crème fraîche in a saucepan. Bring to a boil, then simmer until reduced a little. Add the cubed gorgonzola, and let it melt into the cream. Add the wine and whisk the cream mixture hard using a balloon whisk. Season the sauce with the nutmeg and a little salt to taste. Fold in the chopped walnuts.

10. Put the pasta ribbons in the boiling water, and cook them for a few minutes until *al dente*. Drain the pasta ribbons and transfer them to a large dish. Pour the gorgonzola sauce over them and mix well to ensure the pasta ribbons have a good coating of sauce. Serve the pasta immediately, accompanied by a green salad.

Ravioli
(Maultaschen)

Serves 4

<u>For the pasta:</u>
13 tablespoons bread flour, 2 eggs
½ teaspoon salt, Splash of water
<u>For the filling:</u>
2 slices of stale bread, crusts removed, 1 cup hot milk
1½ pounds ground beef, 4 eggs, beaten
1 bunch of fresh parsley, finely chopped, 1 bunch of fresh dill, finely chopped
1 large onion, peeled and finely chopped, Salt and freshly ground pepper to taste
Freshly grated nutmeg to taste, 4–6 cups hot beef stock

1. <u>For the pasta:</u> Prepare the pasta dough according to the recipe for Homemade Pasta Ribbons on page 96. Allow the dough to rest at room temperature.

2. <u>For the filling:</u> Put the slices of bread in a dish, and pour the hot milk over them. Allow the bread to soak for a few minutes, then drain off the milk and squeeze out the bread.

3. Put the ground beef in a bowl, beat in the bread, the beaten eggs, chopped parsley, chopped dill, and chopped onion. Season the filling generously with salt, pepper, and freshly grated nutmeg.

4. Roll out the pasta dough to form thin sheets about 4 inches wide. Spread the filling evenly over each sheet of pasta. Fold the sheet of pasta over on itself, to form a parcel about 2 inches wide. Cut the pasta parcel into pieces about 2½–3 inches long. Press the sides down firmly, so that the filling does not leak out during cooking. If you like, you can brush the edges of the ravioli with a splash of lightly beaten egg white, to help seal them.

5. Put the beef stock in a saucepan, bring it to a boil, add the ravioli, and cook them at a fast boil for about 6 minutes. Then put a lid on the pan and simmer the ravioli on low heat until cooked through.

6. The ravioli can be served either in the stock, sprinkled with chopped fresh chives, or drained and served au gratin. Ravioli prepared a day in advance is best used in au gratin dishes. Serve sprinkled with crisp, sautéed onions, accompanied by potato salad, and a leafy green salad.

If you replace the ground beef with finely chopped, blanched Savoy cabbage, or cooked sauerkraut, you have vegetarian ravioli, which are sure to delight even non-vegetarians. Because preparing ravioli is a lengthy and laborious process, it is worth making a large quantity and freezing some of them. In this way you always have a soup garnish at hand, or you can quickly prepare a meal of ravioli au gratin.

Rye Käsespätzle with Sauerkraut Salad
(Roggenkäsespätzle mit Sauerkrautsalat)

Serves 2

For the spätzle:
13 tablespoons rye flour, 2 eggs, beaten
1 teaspoon sea salt, Splash of lukewarm water
1 tablespoon olive oil, 1 large red onion, peeled and sliced
3 tablespoons butter, ⅓ cup grated full fat hard cheese, such as Emmenthal
Freshly ground black pepper
For the sauerkraut salad:
1 pound sauerkraut (homemade or store bought), 1 eating apple, grated
1 small red onion, peeled and diced, 1 tablespoon corn oil
Pinch of flavored seasoning pepper to taste

1. <u>For the spätzle:</u> Sift the rye flour into a bowl. Make a well in the center, add the beaten eggs, salt, and a splash of lukewarm water. Using a wooden spoon, work the flour, eggs, and water together to form a smooth, thick batter. Cover and allow it to rest for at least 30 minutes.

2. <u>For the sauerkraut salad:</u> Put the sauerkraut in a large bowl. Add the grated apple, diced onion, and corn oil. Mix them all together thoroughly, and season them with the flavored pepper. Do not add salt to the salad! Put the salad in the refrigerator for about 1 hour, so the flavors can combine.

3. Bring a large saucepan of salted water to a boil. Spread the spätzle batter out over a wooden board. Take a sharp knife, hold it at an angle of 45 degrees to the board, and shave off strips of the mix, letting them drop into the boiling water. Once you have a batch of spätzle in the boiling water, simmer them until they float to the surface. Scoop them out with a slotted spoon, refresh immediately in cold water, and drain in a colander. Repeat this process until all the mixture has been used.

4. Heat the oil in a skillet and sauté the sliced red onion. Add 2 teaspoons of the butter. Melt the remaining butter in another skillet, and toss the spätzle in it. Divide them between two plates, arrange the sautéed onion on top, and sprinkle with the grated cheese and ground pepper. Serve immediately with the sauerkraut salad.

Spätzle made with all-purpose white flour are prepared in exactly the same way. For 4 people, I use 2 cups all-purpose flour, 8 eggs, salt to taste, and a splash of water

Deep-filled Mushroom Quiche
(Champignon-Kuchen)

Serves 4

For the pastry:
13 tablespoons all-purpose flour
Pinch of salt to taste, 2 eggs, beaten
1 tablespoon olive oil
1–2 tablespoons lukewarm water
For the filling:
1 pound button mushrooms, thinly sliced
½ pound tomatoes, ½ pound feta cheese
Butter and dry breadcrumbs for the pan
4 egg yolks, ¾ cup heavy cream
6½ tablespoons freshly grated Parmesan cheese
Salt and freshly ground pepper to taste
1 bunch of fresh thyme, finely chopped
Grated nutmeg, 4 egg whites, stiffly beaten

1. Knead the flour, salt, eggs, olive oil, and water to form a smooth dough. Cover and allow it to rest for 1 hour at room temperature.

2. Immerse the tomatoes in boiling water. Take them out; skin, seed, and dice the flesh.

3. Preheat the oven to 400°F. Roll out the pastry. Butter an 8 inch springform cake pan and dust it with the breadcrumbs. Roll out the pastry into a circle large enough to line the cake pan with a 1½ inch overhang all round.

4. Beat together the egg yolks, cream, Parmesan, salt, pepper, and nutmeg. Add the mushrooms, tomatoes, cubed cheese, and thyme. Fold in the beaten egg whites. Pour the egg mixture into the pastry case. Bake the quiche for 45 minutes, until golden brown.

Spinach Strudel
(Gemüsestrudel)

Serves 4

For the strudel dough:
½ cup lukewarm water
1 egg, beaten, Pinch of salt to taste
2 teaspoons oil, 1 cup bread flour,
For the filling:
2 pounds spinach, 5 tablespoons butter
1 medium-size onion, finely chopped
Salt and freshly grated nutmeg to taste
6½ tablespoons fresh breadcrumbs
¾ cup sour cream

1. For the strudel dough: Make the strudel dough according to the recipe on page 76.

2. For the filling: Carefully wash the spinach leaves, and drain well. Bring a saucepan of water to a boil. Blanch the spinach briefly, drain it, and refresh it in cold water. Chop the spinach roughly in a food processor.

3. Preheat the oven to 350°F. Melt the butter in a saucepan and sauté the onion. Add the spinach and cook until the spinach has wilted and all the liquid has evaporated. Season to taste with salt and nutmeg.

4. Stretch out the strudel dough on a large, floured cloth, following the method on page 76. Sprinkle the breadcrumbs over the strudel dough, and spread the spinach on top. Using the cloth, roll up the strudel, tuck in the ends, and transfer it to a buttered roasting pan. Brush the strudel with some of the sour cream. Transfer it to the oven and bake for 45 minutes, brushing with additional sour cream during cooking.

Asparagus au Gratin
(Überbackener Spargel)

Serves 4

2 pounds asparagus
Salt to taste
8 teaspoons butter
1 tablespoon diced onion
8 teaspoons flour
1 cup hot vegetable stock
1 cup heavy cream
2 tablespoons freshly grated Cheddar cheese
2 egg yolks, beaten
2 egg whites, stiffly beaten

1. Peel the asparagus, and cut it into batons of equal length. Bring a saucepan of salted water to a boil, add the asparagus, and cook for about 20 minutes, until tender. Butter an ovenproof dish. Preheat the oven to 350°F. Drain the asparagus, and place it in the buttered dish.

2. Melt the butter in a saucepan and sauté the onion until translucent. Sprinkle the flour onto the butter and cook it until it foams. Add the hot stock, stirring constantly. Add the cream, continue stirring the sauce, and cook until it thickens. Fold the cheese into the sauce and season with salt. Fold in the egg yolks and finally the stiffly beaten egg whites. Pour the sauce over the asparagus. Bake for 45 minutes until golden brown.

Deep-fried Cauliflower in Beer Batter
(Gebackener Blumenkohl im Bierteig)

Serves 4

1 large cauliflower
Salt to taste
For the beer batter:
1 cup all-purpose flour
1 cup beer
1 tablespoon corn oil
Salt to taste
2 egg yolks
2 egg whites, stiffly beaten
Corn oil for frying

1. Divide the cauliflower into small florets. Bring a saucepan of salted water to a boil and cook the cauliflower until just tender.

2. Sift the flour into a bowl. Make a well in the center, add the beer, oil, salt to taste, and egg yolks. Beat until a smooth batter forms. Fold in the beaten egg whites. Heat the oil to 400°F in a deep-fat fryer or deep saucepan.

3. Dip the cauliflower in the batter until coated all over, then fry immediately in the hot oil until golden brown. Serve with one of the spicy dressings or sauces from pages 26–30 and a crisp, green salad.

Celeriac is also very good for deep-fat frying. It should also be boiled until just tender and coated in batter.

Bavarian Cabbage
(Bayerisches Weißkraut)

Serves 4

1 white cabbage, weighing about 2 pounds
1 medium onion
1 tablespoon clarified butter
Pinch of sugar to taste
1½ cups vegetable stock or water
Salt to taste
1 teaspoon caraway seeds
1 tablespoon all-purpose flour, or 1 small potato, grated
3–4 tablespoons dry white wine

1. Remove the outer leaves from the cabbage. Cut it into quarters, wash, and remove the hard core. Cut the quarters into thin ribbons, or grate them. Peel and finely dice the onion.

2. Melt the clarified butter, add the sugar, and let it caramelize slightly. Add the diced onion and chopped cabbage, and sweat the vegetables in the butter.

3. Add the stock or water, season the cabbage with salt, and add the caraway seeds. Simmer the cabbage on low heat for 1 hour, stirring frequently.

4. Mix the flour with a little water, and use it to thicken the cabbage, or add the grated potato. This step is optional, because the cabbage juices may have created a sauce that is already sufficiently thick. Flavor the cabbage with the white wine.

Braised cabbage tastes even better when reheated.

Braised Red Cabbage
(Blaukraut)

Serves 4

1 red cabbage, weighing about 2 pounds
2 ripe eating apples
1 large onion
1 tablespoon clarified butter
2 teaspoons sugar
⅓ cup red wine vinegar
Salt to taste
3–4 tablespoons red wine

1. Remove the outer leaves from the cabbage. Cut into quarters, wash, and remove the hard core. Cut the quarters into thin ribbons, or grate them.

2. Peel, core, and grate the apples. Peel and dice the onion.

3. Melt the clarified butter in a saucepan, add the sugar, and let it caramelize slightly. Add the grated apple, diced onion, and shredded cabbage, and sweat them briefly. Add the vinegar and season the cabbage with salt. Add a splash of water. Simmer the cabbage on low heat for 1 hour. Flavor the cabbage with the red wine at the end of cooking.

Finger Noodles
(Fingernudeln)

Serves 4

Version I:
2 cups all-purpose flour, Scant cup of hot water
Salt to taste, 6½ tablespoons clarified butter
2 eggs, beaten, 3 tablespoons fresh breadcrumbs
Version II:
2 cups all-purpose flour, 1 ounce yeast
1 cup lukewarm milk, Pinch of sugar to taste
2 eggs, beaten, Pinch of salt to taste
8 teaspoons butter, melted, 1 recipe Gorgonzola Sauce (see page 96)

1. Version I: Sift the flour into a bowl, add the water and a pinch of salt. Work the mixture to form a smooth dough. Shape it into small, thin, finger-length noodles (worms).

2. Bring a large saucepan of salted water to a boil and cook the pasta for about 10 minutes. Drain and refresh in cold water.

3. Preheat the oven to 400°F. Melt the clarified butter in a skillet and toss the pasta in it.

4. Transfer the pasta to an ovenproof dish. Pour the beaten eggs over the pasta, and sprinkle the breadcrumbs on top. Bake until the breadcrumbs are crisp and golden brown. Serve with sauerkraut.

1. Version II: Sift the flour into a bowl. Make a well in the center. Put the crumbled yeast, lukewarm milk, and a pinch of sugar in the well. Mix all the ingredients together. Sprinkle a little flour on top of the mixture, and leave it to rise in a warm place for about 30 minutes.

2. Add the beaten eggs and a pinch of salt, and work the mixture to form a stiff dough. Shape it into thin, finger-length "worms".

3. Brush an ovenproof dish with 2 teaspoons of the melted butter. Arrange a layer of pasta lengthwise in the dish. Brush with more melted butter, then arrange another layer of pasta on top crosswise, to form a lattice. Leave the pasta to rise for 30 minutes in a warm place.

4. Preheat the oven to 350°F. Pour the Gorgonzola Sauce over the pasta. Bake on the middle oven shelf until the sauce is golden brown and bubbling.

If you like sweet pasta, pour sugared milk over the yeast dough fingers, and bake in the oven until golden brown.

Topfennudeln
(Topfennudeln)

Serves 4

1 pound low fat cottage cheese
1 egg, beaten
1½ ounces yeast, crumbled or
1½ envelopes dry yeast
1–2 teaspoons salt
1½ pounds bread flour
Corn oil or clarified butter for deep frying

1. Put the cottage cheese in a large bowl. Add the beaten egg, dry yeast, salt, and half the flour. Work the ingredients until combined, then knead to form a smooth dough. Cover the bowl with a damp cloth and leave the dough to rise in a warm place.

2. When the dough has doubled in size, knock it back, and knead in the rest of the flour.

3. Using a spoon, break off portions of dough, and shape them into finger-width noodles. Heat the oil or clarified butter to 350°F in a deep-fat fryer or deep saucepan, and fry the noodles in batches until golden brown.

4. In Lower Bavaria, these finger noodles are accompanied by sauerkraut or braised Savoy cabbage in a sauce.

Unfortunately, it is not always easy to get the right type of ricotta cheese for this recipe. Most readily-available cottage cheese contains too much liquid, so it is a good idea to drain it through a sieve before you use it.

Potato Noodles
(Kartoffelnudeln)

Serves 4

2 pounds baking potatoes such as Idaho
Salt to taste
1½ –2 cups all-purpose flour
2 eggs, beaten
1 teaspoon salt
Oil for deep frying

1. Peel the potatoes, rinse, and cook in just enough salted water to cover them. Drain them, let the steam evaporate completely, then mash thoroughly, or push through a potato ricer.

2. Combine the mashed potato with the flour, beaten eggs, and salt. Quickly work the ingredients together to form a stiff dough.

3. Lightly dust a pastry board or work surface with flour. Shape the potato mixture into finger-length noodles. Heat plenty of oil to 350°F in a deep-fat fryer or deep saucepan. Deep fry batches of the noodles until golden brown. Serve with sauerkraut or Bavarian Cabbage (see recipe page 101).

The potato noodles will be especially fluffy if you substitute drained cottage cheese for half the quantity of potato. If you don't particularly like cabbage, either of these dishes can be served with a green salad.

Potato Strudels
(Kartoffelstrudel)

Serves 4

For the dough:
2 pounds baking potatoes such as Idaho
1½ –2 cups all-purpose flour
2 eggs, beaten, 1 teaspoon salt
For the filling:
1 pound porcini mushrooms
8 teaspoons butter
1 onion, diced
Salt to taste
½ bunch of fresh parsley, finely chopped
1 cup sour cream
6–8 tablespoons butter, melted

1. Make a potato dough according to the method for Potato Noodles on page 103.

2. Wipe the mushrooms carefully and slice them thin. Melt the butter in a skillet and sauté the diced onion until translucent. Add the mushrooms and sauté until all the liquid has evaporated. Season with salt and stir in the chopped parsley. Set the mixture aside to cool. Preheat the oven to 350°F.

3. Divide the potato dough into 8 equal portions, and roll each one out on a floured pastry board, until you have eight thin pastry rounds. Spread each circle with sour cream, cover with a layer of mushrooms, and roll up.

4. Brush a roasting pan with half the melted butter and arrange the strudels side by side. Brush with melted butter. Bake until golden brown, brushing occasionally with the remaining melted butter. Serve with a salad.

Potato Cake
(Kartoffeldotsch)

Serves 4

10 large baking potatoes
1–2 tablespoons all-purpose flour
1 egg, beaten
½ cup sour cream or heavy cream
1–2 teaspoons salt
Freshly ground pepper to taste
2 tablespoons butter

1. Peel the potatoes and grate them fine. Put them in a sieve and let them drain into a bowl. Reserve the potato juices but do not squeeze out the potato.

2. Put the grated potato in a bowl. Carefully drain off the watery part of the reserved potato juices, and add the starch that has settled to the grated potato. Fold the flour, beaten egg, and sour cream into the potato, and season the mixture generously with salt and pepper.

3. Preheat the oven to 350°F. Melt the butter in an ovenproof dish and add all the potato mixture at once. Press down the surface of the potato mixture. Bake in the middle of the oven for about 30 minutes. Serve immediately with a green salad.

The potato cake should be dark brown only on the underside. If the top is browning too quickly, cover the dish with foil, otherwise the potato cake will be too dry and hard, and will lose much of its delicious flavor.

Mashed Potatoes
(Kartoffelbrei)

Serves 4

2 pounds baking potatoes
Salt to taste
⅓ cup butter
1¼–1⅔ cups heavy cream, warmed
Freshly grated nutmeg to taste
2 tablespoons fresh breadcrumbs

1. Peel the potatoes and cut them into quarters. Boil in just enough salted water to cover them, until soft. Drain the potatoes, let the steam evaporate, and immediately mash them, or push them through a potato ricer into the hot pan.

2. Add 2 tablespoons of butter and enough cream to make a smooth paste, stirring all the time. Season with salt and nutmeg to taste. Take the prepared mashed potatoes off the heat.

3. Melt the remaining butter in a skillet until foaming and sauté the breadcrumbs until they are crisp and golden. Transfer the mashed potatoes to a serving dish and pour the hot butter and fried breadcrumbs over them.

If you like your mashed potatoes more savory, top them with caramelized, sautéed onions. Strange as it may sound, all my life I have liked eating mashed potatoes with stewed pears!

Potato Pudding
(Kartoffelpudding)

Serves 4

2 pounds baking potatoes such as Idaho
Salt to taste
⅓ cup butter
1-1½ cups cream, warmed
Freshly grated nutmeg to taste
10 tablespoons freshly grated Emmenthal cheese
Butter and dry breadcrumbs for the soufflé dish
1 large bunch of fresh watercress

1. Prepare the Mashed Potatoes as in the recipe above, but use a little less cream.

2. Fold the grated cheese into the potato mixture. Butter a soufflé dish and dust it with the breadcrumbs. Transfer the potato mixture to the soufflé dish.

3. Preheat the oven to 250–275 °F. Stand the dish in a roasting pan. Fill the pan with hot water until it comes halfway up the sides of the dish. Put the pan in the oven and bake the potato pudding for about 45 minutes. Check the roasting pan occasionally to be sure the water has not evaporated and add more hot water as necessary.

4. Take the soufflé dish out of the roasting pan. Turn the potato pudding out onto a serving dish and surround it with a garnish of fresh watercress.

Potato Dumplings
(Rohe Kartoffelknödel)

Serves 4

3–3½ pounds potatoes, 2 slices dry white bread, crusts removed
8 teaspoons clarified butter, 1 pound potatoes, boiled in their skins
1½ cups boiling milk, 1 tablespoon salt

1. Peel the raw potatoes and grate them fine into a bowl of cold water.

2. Pour the grated potato into a linen bag or a clean kitchen towel and squeeze it out well, reserving the potato juices.

3. Cut the bread into small cubes. Melt the clarified butter in a skillet and sauté the bread cubes until golden brown. Allow them to cool a little.

4. Peel the boiled potatoes. Grate them fine, or push them through a potato ricer.

5. Put the grated raw potato in a large bowl. Carefully drain off the liquid from the potato juices. Add the potato starch, that has separated out to the raw potato and mix

thoroughly. Pour the boiling milk over the raw potato and season with salt. Add the grated, boiled potato and allow the mixture to cool for a few minutes. Knead all the ingredients together quickly to form a smooth dough.

6. Dampen your hands and shape portions of the potato mixture into tennis ball-sized dumplings. Insert some croutons into the middle of each dumpling, cover them with more potato, and shape the dumpling into a ball again. Bring a large saucepan of salted water to a boil. Add the dumplings to the pan. Put a lid on the pan, turn the heat to low, and simmer gently for about 30 minutes.

7. Remove from the water with a slotted spoon, and drain well. Serve immediately.

Boiled Potato Dumplings
(Gekochte Kartoffelknödel)

Serves 4

2 pounds boiled baking potatoes such as Idaho
1 cup potato flour
1–2 teaspoons salt
1–2 cups boiling water
1 slice stale bread, crust removed
4 teaspoons clarified butter

1. Peel the boiled potatoes while they are still hot and push them through a potato ricer. Allow the riced potatoes to cool a little, then sprinkle the potato flour over them, season with salt, and pour the boiling water over all. Mix the ingredients together quickly, then knead them to form a smooth dough.

2. Cut the bread slice into small cubes. Melt the clarified butter in a skillet and sauté the bread cubes until golden brown.

3. Dust your hands lightly with flour. Shape portions of the potato dough into tennis ball-sized dumplings. Make a hollow in the middle of each and insert some of the croutons. Cover the hollow with more potato mixture, and shape into a ball again.

4. Bring a large saucepan of salted water to a boil. Put the dumplings in the boiling water, bring to a boil again, and simmer for 20 minutes on a low heat.

This kind of dumpling tastes especially good with sauerbraten. The potato mixture must be fairly stiff, otherwise the dumplings fall apart when poached.

Potato Pancakes
(Kartoffelpuffer)

Serves 4

2 pounds waxy potatoes
2 eggs, beaten
2–4 tablespoons flour
1 cup sour cream
Salt to taste
Corn oil for sautéing

1. Peel the potatoes and grate them fine. Put the grated potato in a sieve and leave it to drain, collecting the juices in a bowl. Drain off the watery liquid. Add the potato starch, that has separated out to the grated potato and mix well.

2. Add the beaten eggs, flour, sour cream, and salt, and mix to form a smooth batter.

3. Heat plenty of oil in a skillet. Place tablespoons of potato batter in the hot oil. Press the batter down with the back of a spoon and sauté on one side until golden brown. Turn the pancakes and sauté them on the other side until crisp and golden. Continue until all the potato batter is used up. These pancakes are best enjoyed hot from the skillet.

The accompaniment to potato pancakes varies greatly, not only from region to region but also from family to family. The range extends from apple sauce to cranberries to sauerkraut to Bolognese sauce.

Bread Dumplings
(Semmelknödel)

Serves 4

10 slices stale white bread, crusts removed
2 cups hot milk
1 tablespoon chopped fresh parsley
2 tablespoons diced onion
2–3 eggs, beaten
Salt to taste

1. Put the slices of bread in a dish, pour the hot milk over them, and leave to soak for about 15 minutes.

2. Add the chopped parsley, diced onion, and beaten eggs to the bread. Season with salt, and mix quickly to form a smooth paste. If the mixture is too soft, add some more bread or a couple of tablespoons of flour.

3. Bring a large saucepan of salted water to a boil.

4. Dampen your hands and use them to shape portions of the bread mixture into dumplings. Put them in the boiling water. Simmer on a low heat for 15–20 minutes, with the pan half covered. Remove from the water with a slotted spoon and allow to drain thoroughly. Serve immediately.

Chop 3–4 slices of bacon and sauté it until crisp. Add the chopped bacon to the dumplings with the parsley, onion, and eggs to make savory bacon dumplings, which can be served in a strong consommé.

Bread Pudding
(Semmelpudding)

Serves 4

10 slices stale white bread, crusts removed
1½ cups hot milk
¼ cup butter, softened, 4 eggs, beaten
1 tablespoon chopped fresh dill
2 tablespoons diced onion
2–4 tablespoons freshly grated Cheddar cheese
1 teaspoon salt
Butter and dry breadcrumbs for the baking dish

1. Put the slices of bread in a dish, pour the milk over them, and leave to soak for 15 minutes.

2. Beat the softened butter until light and fluffy, then gradually beat in the soaked bread and the eggs. Add the chopped dill, diced onion, and grated cheese, and season to taste with salt.

3. Preheat the oven to 350°F. Butter a pudding basin and dust it with the breadcrumbs. Transfer the bread mixture to the basin. Stand it in a roasting pan, and fill the pan with hot water until it comes halfway up the sides of the basin. Steam the pudding for 1–1¼ hours. Check the roasting pan occasionally and add more hot water as necessary.

4. Take the pudding out of the oven. Turn it out onto a warm serving dish. Serve as an accompaniment to a meat dish or as a main course with a side salad.

You can increase the amount of cheese, and you could also add 3 ounces of diced boiled ham to the pudding.

Semolina Dumplings
(Abgerührte Grießklöße)

Serves 4

2 cups milk, 3½ tablespoons butter
14 tablespoons durum wheat semolina
3–4 slices stale white bread, crusts removed
4 eggs, beaten, Salt to taste

1. Pour the milk into a saucepan, bring it to a boil, and melt 4 teaspoons of butter in it. Pour the semolina into the hot milk, stirring all the time, and cook it over a medium heat, stirring constantly, until a firm porridge results. Allow the porridge to cool.

2. Cut the bread slices into small cubes. Melt the remaining butter in a skillet and sauté the bread until the cubes are crisp and golden brown.

3. Fold the croutons into the cooled porridge, gradually beat in the eggs, and stir the mixture until it forms a workable dough.

4. Bring a large saucepan of salted water to a boil. Shape the semolina mixture into small dumplings and drop them into the boiling water. Bring the water to a boil again, then simmer on low heat for 10–15 minutes. Remove from the pan with a slotted spoon and drain well.

These semolina dumplings go very well with game and mushroom sauce. The sweet variation of the recipe is popular with adults and children alike. The dumplings are rolled in sugar and cinnamon and served with stewed prunes.

Schuxen
(Schuxen)

Serves 4

1 pound rye flour, or ½ pound rye flour and ½ pound white bread flour
1 teaspoon salt
1½ ounces fresh or dry yeast (check yeast-to-flour ratio on packet)
Pinch of sugar to taste, ½ cup warmed milk
Clarified butter for frying

1. Put the flour and salt in a bowl and make a well in the center. Put the yeast, a pinch of sugar, and the milk in the well. Work a little of the flour into the milk and yeast mixture. Sprinkle a pinch of flour over the top of the yeast mixture. Leave it in a warm place to rise for 30 minutes.

2. Work the mixture until it forms a smooth, fairly firm yeast dough. Cover the dough and allow it to rise for 1 hour.

3. Cut off small portions of the dough and roll them out into small rounds. Cover and leave to rise for a few minutes.

4. Melt lots of clarified butter in a deep-fat fryer or deep saucepan, and heat it to 400°F.

5. Fry batches of the *Schuxen* until golden brown and crisp.

Schuxen *are the traditional accompaniment to the simple Lower Bavarian Potato Soup (see page 45). They are also good with mushroom dishes, or sprinkled with cinnamon and sugar and served with stewed plums or apples.*

I find it hard to resist sweet temptations, and I don't try to make excuses for myself. I quite happily admit that, to me, a meal is not complete without dessert. In our house, even the most modest meal ends with a small dessert, even if it's just a fruit compote. We just have to have that sweet finishing touch.

The desserts I prepare are governed by the time of year. To me, there is nothing more delicious in May than ripe strawberries, sometimes with cream, sometimes with ice cream. In the early summer months I prepare lots of refreshing desserts based on soft fruit. In summer I like using apricots, but only when they are fully ripe. The occasional apple strudel at apple-picking time is almost obligatory, and in winter we often round off our meals with a steamed pudding, or occasionally with a few pancakes. If I don't have time to prepare a dessert in advance, I at least have a cup of coffee, or a freshly brewed cup of tea, with a few cookies. I bake all year round, not just at Christmas, and therefore always have a few cookies in the cupboard.

Bread Pudding with Sabayon Sauce
(Mutschelpudding mit Weinschaumsauce)

Serves 4

For the pudding:
6 eggs, 6 egg yolks
1 cup sugar, Grated zest of ½ lemon
½ cup ground almonds
⅔ cup very fine, fresh breadcrumbs
Butter and dry breadcrumbs for the basin
For the sabayon sauce:
1 cup medium white wine, 3–4 egg yolks
1 teaspoon cornstarch, Sugar to taste
Juice of ½ lemon, 3–4 egg whites, stiffly beaten

1. Whisk together the eggs, egg yolks, and sugar until thick and foamy. Fold in the lemon zest, almonds, and breadcrumbs. Preheat the oven to 400°F. Butter a pudding basin or soufflé dish, and dust it with the dry breadcrumbs. Transfer the pudding mixture to the basin. Stand it in a roasting pan, and fill the pan with hot water to come halfway up the sides of the basin. Steam the pudding for 1 hour. Check the roasting pan occasionally, and add more hot water as necessary.

2. Whisk together the white wine, egg yolks, cornstarch, and sugar in a bowl set over a saucepan of simmering water. Add the lemon juice and, whisking the sauce continually with a balloon whisk, bring it slowly to a boil. Take it off the heat, and pour it into a china bowl. Stand the bowl in ice-cold water and continue whisking the sauce until it is completely cold. Fold in the stiffly beaten egg whites. Take the pudding out of the oven and turn it out onto a serving dish. Serve with the sabayon sauce.

Soufflé Grand Marnier
(Soufflé Grand Marnier)

Serves 4

8 teaspoons butter
3 tablespoons all-purpose flour
Pinch of salt to taste
1 cup milk
5 egg yolks
⅓ cup Grand Marnier
2 teaspoons vanilla sugar
5 egg whites
4 teaspoons superfine granulated sugar
Butter and sugar for the ramekins

1. Melt the butter in a saucepan. Add the flour and a pinch of salt to taste, stirring constantly to prevent lumps forming.

2. Gradually add the milk to the *roux*, stirring all the time. The thicker the sauce, the better the soufflé will be. Preheat the oven to 400°F.

3. Take the saucepan off the heat. Gradually beat in the egg yolks, Grand Marnier, and vanilla sugar. Beat the egg whites and superfine granulated sugar together until very stiff. Lightly fold the beaten egg whites into the soufflé mixture.

4. Butter 4 individual ramekins and dust them with sugar. Fill with the soufflé mixture. Put in the oven and bake for 10 minutes. Reduce the heat to 350°F and continue baking until they have risen and are golden brown. Serve the soufflés in the ramekins, with fruit compote or fresh strawberries.

Almond Pudding with Rosehip Sauce
(Mandelpudding mit Hagebuttensauce)

Serves 4

<u>For the almond pudding:</u>
½ pound almonds, shelled, ¾ stick butter, softened
6½ tablespoons superfine granulated sugar, 5 egg yolks
8 teaspoons fresh breadcrumbs, 5 egg whites
Butter and dry breadcrumbs for the dish
<u>For the rosehip sauce:</u>
5 cups medium white wine, 3½ tablespoons superfine granulated sugar
4 tablespoons rosehip, or raspberry purée
3 egg yolks, 3 tablespoons superfine granulated sugar

1. <u>For the almond pudding:</u> Toast the almonds in a skillet until they are golden brown and toasted. Allow them to cool, then grind them fine.

2. Beat together the softened butter and ⅓ cup of the sugar. Gradually add the egg yolks, stirring constantly, until the mixture is light and fluffy. Fold in the ground almonds and the breadcrumbs. Beat together the egg whites and the remaining sugar until stiff. Fold into the pudding mixture.

3. Preheat the oven to 400°F. Butter a pudding basin or soufflé dish, and dust it with breadcrumbs. Transfer the almond mixture to the basin. Stand the basin in a roasting pan. Fill the pan with hot water to come halfway up the sides of the basin. Put the pudding in the oven and cook for 45 minutes. Check the roasting pan occasionally to be sure the water has not evaporated and add more hot water as necessary.

4. <u>For the sauce:</u> Put the wine and sugar in a saucepan and bring it to a boil. In a clean saucepan, beat together the rosehip, or raspberry purée, egg yolks, and sugar until frothy. Gradually add the wine, whisking the sauce quick and hard, over a medium heat. Take the sauce off the heat and allow the flavors to infuse.

5. Take the pudding out of the oven and turn it out onto a warm serving dish. Serve with the rosehip, or raspberry sauce.

Rheinischer Bund
(Rheinischer Bund)

Serves 4

5 egg yolks
1 tablespoon cornstarch
6½ tablespoons superfine granulated sugar
Juice and grated zest of 1 lemon
1 cup white wine
20 almond macaroons
5 egg whites
¼ cup superfine granulated sugar
3½ tablespoons ground almonds

1. Put the egg yolks, cornstarch, 6 ½ table-spoons of sugar, lemon juice, lemon zest, and white wine in a saucepan. Cook the egg mixture over medium heat, whisking all the time, until thick and frothy. Pour into a long, deep dish, smooth the surface, and allow to cool.

2. Cover the custard thickly with bought, or homemade (see recipe page 144) almond macaroons.

3. Preheat the oven to 425°F. Beat the egg whites until stiff, gradually adding the ½ cup sugar in a slow trickle. Continue beating until the egg whites are glossy and very stiff. Spread the meringue over the macaroons and sprinkle the ground almonds on top.

4. Bake the meringue in the hot oven until golden brown. Serve immediately.

Apple Charlotte
(Apfelcharlotte)

Serves 4

6–7 large cooking apples
1 cup white wine
3½ tablespoons superfine granulated sugar
1 cinnamon stick
3½ tablespoons sultanas
1 loaf stale white bread (at least 2 days old)
1 ¼ sticks butter, melted
1 cup heavy cream, stiffly whipped

1. Peel, quarter, and core the apples. Slice them thin.

2. Put the white wine in a saucepan with the sugar, cinnamon, and sultanas, and bring to a boil. Lower the heat, add the sliced apples and simmer until the apples are just tender. The apple slices should remain whole. Allow to cool.

3. Preheat the oven to 350°F. Cut the crusts off the white bread and cut it into ¼ inch thick slices. Dip the bread in the melted butter and use the slices to line an ovenproof baking dish. Cover with the stewed apple mixture and top with the remaining slices of butter-soaked bread to form a lid. Bake the charlotte for 45 minutes.

4. Allow the charlotte to cool, then cover it with a layer of whipped cream. Refrigerate for 2 hours before serving.

Depending on the time of year, you can substitute apricots, pears, or plums for the apples. The stewed fruit should be completely cold before you spread it over the bread.

Kaiserschmarrn
(Kaiserschmarrn)

Serves 4

1¼ cup all-purpose flour
3 egg yolks
1½ cups milk
½ cup sour cream
¼ teaspoon vanilla extract
Pinch of salt to taste
3 egg whites
½–¾ stick butter, melted
2–3 tablespoons superfine granulated sugar
Handful of sultanas or toasted almonds to taste

1. Beat together the flour, egg yolks, milk, sour cream, vanilla extract, and salt, to form a smooth pancake batter. Beat the egg whites until stiff and fold them into the batter.

2. Brush a skillet with some of the melted butter. Pour all of the batter in the pan. Sauté on medium heat until golden brown.

3. Using two forks, break the pancake into pieces. Sprinkle the sugar over it and drizzle the remaining melted butter on top.

4. Keeping the pan moving all the time, let the pieces of pancake caramelize in the butter and sugar. Sprinkle the sultanas or toasted almonds on top and serve immediately.

Cranberries and apple sauce go very well with these pancakes.

Carthusian Dumplings
(Karthäuserklöße)

Serves 4

2 egg yolks
2 tablespoons sugar
1 cup milk
8 bread rolls, broken up
2 egg whites
6½ tablespoons fresh breadcrumbs
Corn oil for deep frying
2–3 tablespoons superfine granulated sugar
½ teaspoon ground cinnamon

1. Beat together the egg yolks, sugar, and milk. Add the bread and soak until all the liquid has been absorbed.

2. Beat the egg whites with 1 tablespoon of water. Dip the bread in the egg whites, then toss in the breadcrumbs. Press the breadcrumbs down well onto the rolls.

3. Heat lots of oil in a skillet, and sauté the "dumplings" in it, until crisp and golden brown on both sides. Mix together the sugar and cinnamon. Toss the "dumplings" in the sugar mixture while still hot. Serve with a fruit compote.

"Drunken Maiden" (Versoffene Jungfern) is prepared in a similar way. The bread rolls, crusts removed, are soaked in red wine flavored with cinnamon and sugar. They are then coated in breadcrumbs and sautéed.

Sabayon Trifle
(Weincreme)

Serves 4

2–3 tablespoons sultanas
5 tablespoons brandy
6 eggs
2 cups white wine
Pinch of ground cinnamon to taste
1 envelope unflavored gelatin
1 cup heavy cream, stiffly whipped
Lady fingers
Small almond macaroons

1. Rinse the sultanas. Soak them in the brandy for at least 15 minutes.

2. Put the eggs, white wine, and cinnamon in a metal bowl. Set the bowl over a pan of simmering water and whisk the sabayon until the mixture starts to froth and thicken.

3. Dissolve the unflavored gelatin in hot water and fold it carefully into the sabayon sauce. Refrigerate the custard. Just before it starts to set, fold in half the whipped cream.

4. Line the sides of a glass dish with lady fingers biscuits. Put half the custard in the dish and cover it with a layer of macaroons. Cover the macaroons with the brandy-soaked sultanas and the remaining custard. Refrigerate for at least 2 hours to set.

5. Just before serving garnish the trifle with the remaining whipped cream.

Lemon Mousse
(Zitronencreme)

Serves 4

4 egg yolks
6½ tablespoons superfine granulated sugar
Juice of 2 lemons
1½ cups apple juice
1 envelope unflavored gelatin
4 egg whites
1 cup heavy cream

1. Beat together the egg yolks and 4 teaspoons of the sugar until frothy. Gradually add the lemon juice and apple juice, whisking all the time, and continue whisking hard until a thick, frothy custard forms.

2. Dissolve the unflavored gelatin in hot water and add it to the custard drop by drop, whisking all the time. Refrigerate until the custard starts to set.

3. Beat the egg whites and the remaining sugar until very stiff. Whip the cream until stiff. Fold the beaten egg whites and whipped cream into the custard. Transfer to a serving dish, or individual dishes, and return to the refrigerator to set completely.

I usually prepare this citrus mousse without the cream. Instead, I flavor the cream with vanilla and serve it separately with the mousse.

Bavarian Mousse with Pumpernickel

(Bayerische Creme mit Pumpernickel)

Serves 4

¼ pound pumpernickel bread
1 cup milk
10 tablespoons superfine granulated sugar
2½ tablespoons kirsch liqueur
3 egg yolks
2 cups heavy cream
1 teaspoon vanilla extract
1 envelope unflavored gelatin
3 egg whites, stiffly beaten

1. Crumble the pumpernickel into a bowl. Put the milk and 3½ tablespoons of the sugar in a saucepan, bring to a boil, and pour over the pumpernickel. Drizzle the kirsch over the bread. Mix all the ingredients together thoroughly. Cover and allow to marinate for 4 hours.

2. Put the egg yolks and the remaining sugar in a saucepan. Whisk them together thoroughly over medium heat. Add half the cream and the vanilla, and continue to whisk until thick and foamy. Bring the custard to a boil, then immediately pour it into a china bowl.

3. Dissolve the unflavored gelatin in a little hot water and add it to the custard. Stir well, allow the mixture to cool, then refrigerate.

4. Whip the remaining cream until very stiff. When the custard is nearly set, whisk it, then fold in the stiffly beaten egg whites and the whipped cream.

5. Fold the pumpernickel mixture into the mousse. Cover and refrigerate for 3 hours.

6. If you want to turn out the mousse, you will need to refrigerate it for at least 6 hours.

Bavarian Mousse can be adapted to suit your taste. Classic Rahmsulz, *as it is commonly known in Bavaria, is also prepared without pumpernickel, turned out, and served with fresh berries or a seasonal fruit compote.*

Mocha-Rum Mousse
(Mokka-Rumcreme)

Serves 4

5 egg yolks
½ cup confectioners' sugar
4 teaspoons vanilla-flavored sugar
1 tablespoon cocoa powder
½ cup cold, strong Mocha-Java coffee
6 tablespoons rum
1 envelope unflavored gelatin
5 egg whites
1 cup heavy cream

1. Whisk the egg yolks and confectioner's sugar together until frothy. Gradually add the vanilla sugar, cocoa powder, coffee, and rum, whisking all the time. Continue whisking until the custard is thick and frothy.

2. Dissolve the unflavored gelatin in a little hot water and carefully stir into the custard. Refrigerate until the custard begins to set.

3. Beat the egg whites until stiff. Whip the cream until very stiff. Gently fold the egg whites and cream into the custard. Transfer the mousse to a large glass dish, or individual dishes. Allow the mousse to set for several hours in the refrigerator.

The mousse looks pretty if garnished with rosettes of whipped cream and chocolate-coated coffee beans.

Cranberry Mousse
(Preiselbeercreme)

Serves 4

2 egg yolks
2–3 tablespoons cold milk
1 teaspoon cornstarch
1 cup heavy cream
2 egg whites
½ cup superfine granulated sugar
6 tablespoons cranberries in syrup

1. Put the egg yolks, milk, and cornstarch in a saucepan, and blend them together until smooth. Add the cream and cook the custard mixture over medium heat, stirring all the time, until it comes to a boil.

2. Pour the custard into a china bowl. Stand the bowl in ice-cold water and stir until the custard is completely cold. Then put the custard in the refrigerator and allow it to set.

3. Beat the egg whites, gradually drizzling in the sugar. Continue beating until they are very firm and glossy.

4. Fold the cranberries into the meringue mixture, then fold in spoonfuls of the custard. Transfer the mousse to individual dishes and refrigerate.

You can substitute raspberry or blackcurrant jelly for the cranberries.

Creme à la Nesselrode
(Creme à la Nesselrode)

Serves 4

½ pound chestnuts, ½ vanilla bean, slit open
1 cup milk, 1 cup heavy cream
6 egg yolks, 1 cup superfine granulated sugar
1 envelope unflavored gelatin, 2 tablespoons Maraschino
½ cup sultanas, ¼ cup raisins
¼ cup candied orange and lemon peel, 2 cups heavy cream, stiffly whipped
Splash of almond oil to taste

1. Score a cross in the top of each chestnut. Place them on a baking sheet and bake in a hot oven until the shells start to peel back. Allow to cool. Shell them and put them in a saucepan with the vanilla bean and the milk. Bring to a boil, then cook the chestnuts on low heat until tender. Take the vanilla bean out of the milk and scrape out the seeds. Transfer the chestnuts and milk to a blender or food processor, add the vanilla extract and purée them. Push the mixture through a sieve and allow it to cool.

2. Put the cream, egg yolks, and sugar in a saucepan. Beat them together over medium heat until thick and frothy. Dissolve the unflavored gelatin in a little hot water and add it to the custard, stirring all the time. Remove from the heat and pour into a china bowl. Stand the bowl in ice-cold water and continue beating until the custard is completely cold.

3. Gradually stir in the cooled chestnut purée and continue stirring until it has cooled completely.

4. Fold in the Maraschino, sultanas, raisins, and candied peel. Lightly fold in the whipped cream.

5. Brush the inside of a glass dish with almond oil. Pour the mousse into the dish and refrigerate for several hours until set.

Cinnamon Parfait
(Zimtparfait)

Serves 4

2 egg yolks
6½ tablespoons superfine granulated sugar
1 cup heavy cream
1 teaspoon ground cinnamon

1. Whisk the egg yolks and sugar until frothy. Whip the cream until stiff. Fold the egg mixture and cream together lightly, and flavor with the cinnamon. Pour the cream mixture into a loaf pan, or terrine. Smooth the top, cover it with foil, and freeze for several hours.

2. Remove the parfait from the freezer about 30 minutes before you want to serve it and allow it to stand at room temperature. Turn the parfait out and slice it. A hot prune purée is a delicious accompaniment.

To make the prune purée, rinse 1 pound of prunes, put them in a bowl, and pour 4 cups of red wine over them. The wine should cover the prunes completely. Leave the prunes to macerate for two days at room temperature, adding more red wine as necessary. Transfer the prunes and marinade to a saucepan. Heat until almost to the boiling point, then pour into a blender or food processor and purée. Return the purée to the saucepan, bring to a boil, and simmer briefly to thicken it. Serve the hot prune purée with the parfait.

Strawberry Iced Gateau
(Erdbeer-Eistorte)

Serves 4

1½ pounds strawberries
1 packet nut brittle
4 meringue shells, crumbled
4 cups heavy cream
Superfine granulated sugar to taste
4 teaspoons vanilla-flavored sugar
Squeeze of lemon juice to taste
½ cup heavy cream, whipped

1. Hull 1 pound of the strawberries. Rinse them and purée in a blender or food processor. Stir the nut brittle and crumbled meringues into the purée.

2. Whip the 4 cups of cream until stiff. Flavor the cream with the sugar and vanilla sugar. Carefully fold the strawberry purée into the cream and adjust the flavor to taste with a squeeze of lemon juice.

3. Line a round cake pan or mold with foil. Pour the strawberry cream into the pan. Freeze for several hours.

4. Hull, wash, and slice the remaining strawberries. Take the gateau out of the freezer about 30 minutes before you want to serve it, turn it out onto a plate, and slice it. Serve with the remaining strawberries and the whipped cream.

To me, there is no nicer dessert in May and June than new-season strawberries with cream!

Plum Dumplings
(Zwetschgenknödel)

Serves 4

1 pound all-purpose flour
Salt to taste
4 teaspoons butter
2 egg yolks, beaten
1 cup milk
2 pounds purple plums, washed
Sugar cubes
¼ cup butter, melted
2–3 tablespoons superfine granulated sugar
½ teaspoon cinnamon

1. Sift the flour into a bowl and add a pinch of salt. Rub the butter into the flour. Add the beaten egg yolks and enough milk to form a soft, smooth dough.

2. Push the dough through a sieve with a wooden spoon. Using a tablespoon, break off small portions of dough.

3. Stone the plums, leaving the fruit whole, and replace the stone with a sugar cube. Wrap each plum in a piece of dough, and shape it into a dumpling.

4. Bring a large saucepan of salted water to a boil. Add the plum dumplings and simmer on low heat for 10–15 minutes.

5. Remove the dumplings from the saucepan with a slotted spoon. Arrange the dumplings on a serving platter and pour the melted butter over them. Mix the cinnamon and sugar together and sprinkle it over the dumplings.

Apple Dumplings
(Apfelknödel)

Serves 4

1 cup milk
½ stick + 1 teaspoon butter
9 tablespoons all-purpose flour
Pinch of salt to taste
2 eggs
3 egg yolks
3 ripe dessert apples
4 cups apple juice
2 cups water
2–3 tablespoons superfine granulated sugar
½ teaspoon ground cinnamon

1. Prepare a choux pastry using the milk, butter, flour, salt, eggs, and egg yolks (see recipe page 38).

2. Peel, quarter, and core the apples. Slice them thin on the diagonal. Stir them into the choux paste.

3. Pour the apple juice and water into a medium-size saucepan and bring to a boil. Reduce the heat until the liquid is simmering gently.

4. Using a tablespoon, break off portions of choux pastry, shape them into dumplings, and drop them into the simmering apple juice. Poach for 5–7 minutes.

5. Remove the dumplings from the liquid with a slotted spoon and divide them equally among four plates. Mix the cinnamon and sugar together and sprinkle it over the dumplings.

Apple Fritters
(Apfelkücherl)

Serves 4

6 large ripe dessert apples
12 tablespoons superfine granulated sugar
3 tablespoons Calvados or rum
1¼ cups all-purpose flour
3 egg yolks
1 cup milk, or cider, or beer
3 egg whites
Corn oil for sautéing

1. Peel the apples. Remove the cores, leaving the apples whole, and cut each apple into ½-inch thick slices. Sprinkle 3 tablespoons of the sugar over the sliced apples and drizzle the Calvados or rum over them.

2. Beat together the flour, egg yolks, and your preferred liquid to form a thick batter. Beat the egg whites until stiff, adding 3 tablespoons of the sugar in a slow trickle. Continue beating until the meringue is glossy and very firm. Fold evenly into the batter.

3. Heat the oil to 350°F in a deep-fat fryer.

4. Dip the marinated apple slices in the batter and sauté them in batches until golden brown.

5. Drain the fritters on absorbent kitchen paper. Toss them in sugar. Serve hot.

Never cook too many apple fritters at once because the oil in the deep-fat fryer will cool too much and the batter will soak it up.

Elderflower Fritters
(Holunderkücherl)

Serves 4

15 elderflower blossom sprays
Corn oil for sautéing
Pancake batter (see recipe opposite)
Confectioners' sugar for dusting

1. Leave a little bit of stem on the elderflower sprays, so there is something to get hold of. Carefully swirl the sprays in cold water. Drain them thoroughly on paper towels.

2. Heat the oil to 350°F in a deep-fat fryer, or deep saucepan. Dip the elderflower sprays in the pancake batter and fry them in the hot oil, one at a time.

3. Drain on absorbent kitchen paper and dust with confectioners' sugar. Serve the deep-fried elderflower sprays immediately.

I prefer beer for this batter, because it lends it an interesting flavor.

Russian Oranges
(Russische Orangen)

Serves 4

6 oranges, ½ cup superfine granulated sugar
7 tablespoons rum, 4 egg yolks
1 cup heavy cream

1. Using a sharp knife, peel the oranges so that the white pith is completely removed.

2. Slice the oranges thin. Arrange the slices attractively in a deep glass dish. Sprinkle 8 teaspoons of the sugar over them and drizzle 5 tablespoons of rum on top. Refrigerate the orange slices and allow to marinate for about 2 hours.

3. Whisk the egg yolks and remaining sugar together until frothy. Whip the cream until stiff and fold it into the egg mixture. Refrigerate for 2 hours.

4. Just before serving, flavor the custard with the remaining rum and spread the mixture over the marinated oranges.

This refreshing orange dessert is the perfect end to a rich meal. The custard looks particularly attractive sprinkled with chopped pistachio nuts.

Apricot Jelly
(Aprikosengrütze)

Serves 4

2 pounds ripe apricots
Sugar to taste
2–3 cups white wine, or apricot juice
1 envelope unflavored gelatin
1 cup heavy cream

1. Wash the apricots. Bring a large saucepan of water to a boil. Plunge them into the boiling water for a few seconds, remove and skin them. Halve and stone the apricots and cut them into four or eight segments each. Sprinkle the sugar over them and allow to macerate for at least 1 hour.

2. Put the apricots in a saucepan with the white wine or apricot juice, and bring to a boil. Turn the heat low and cook gently until soft.

3. Dissolve the unflavored gelatin in a little hot water and gradually stir it into the hot, stewed apricots. Transfer the stewed apricots to a dish. When they have cooled, refrigerate them.

4. Serve the apricot jelly with lightly whipped, sweetened cream.

You can make many other fruit jellies in the same way. The one important thing is that the fruit should always be fully ripe and full of flavor.

Fresh Marinated Figs
(Frische marinierte Feigen)

Serves 4

10 fresh figs
5 tablespoons cognac
½ cup Muscatel wine
1 cup heavy cream
4 teaspoons vanilla-flavored sugar

1. Wash the figs carefully. Remove the leaves and stalks. Cut into segments and arrange them prettily on a deep, round dish. Pour the cognac over them, cover, and put in the refrigerator to marinate overnight.

2. Pour the Muscatel wine over the figs, refrigerate again, and allow them to marinate for a few hours.

3. Whip the cream and vanilla sugar until it forms soft peaks. Spread half the cream over the figs just before serving. Pass the remaining cream separately.

It doesn't matter whether you use purple or green figs for this dessert. Purple figs are somewhat sweeter.

A love of baking has been handed down in my family, and if you bake the delicious yeast cake, *Urgroßmutters gerührten Bund* ("Great-grandmother's Yeast Cake"), that I particularly love, you will understand why. Ever since I was a child, I have loved the tempting aroma of a freshly baked yeast cake. To me, it epitomizes coziness and togetherness, which may be another reason why I enjoy baking so much. No wonder I associate many of my recipes with loving family gatherings.

Romantic as baking might be, if you want a successful cake, you have to follow the specified quantities exactly, much more so than in other types of cooking. I have therefore compiled a Basic Recipe for the most common types of cake mixture, dough, etc. I always prepare the fat-free sponge as described for the Jelly Roll (page 128). The Sponge Cake (page 134) shows how I make a regular sponge batter. Shortcrust pastry is explained in the method for Cheesecake (page 136), and there are two suggested methods for yeast dough: In the Nut Ring recipe (page 138), you will find the method for a strong yeast dough, while the method for Great-grandmother's Yeast Cake (page 139) explains a yeast batter.

My family feels Christmas is on the way when we slice the Fruit Bread (page 135). It must be prepared two to three weeks in advance and, packaged in red and gold like an Advent candle, my family thinks it a gift worth having.

Jelly Roll
(Biskuitroulade)

6 egg yolks
½ cup superfine granulated sugar
6 egg whites
7 teaspoons all-purpose flour
7 teaspoons cornstarch
Grated zest of 1 lemon
Raspberry or apricot jelly
Confectioners' sugar for dusting

1. Preheat the oven to 350°F. Beat the egg yolks and sugar together until pale, thick, and frothy. Whisk the egg whites until very stiff.

2. Sift the flour and cornstarch into the egg yolk mixture. Add the lemon zest and mix thoroughly. Carefully fold the egg whites into the mixture.

3. Line a jelly roll pan with baking parchment. Spread the sponge carefully and evenly. Bake for 10 minutes, or until slightly risen and golden brown.

4. Turn the sponge out onto a damp dish cloth. Allow it to cool. Carefully peel off the baking parchment. Using an icing knife, spread the raspberry or apricot jam over the sponge to the thickness you prefer. With the help of the dish cloth, starting from a short end, roll up the sponge. Dust with confectioners' sugar before serving.

Fake Fried Eggs
(Falsche Spiegeleier)

2 jelly roll sponges (see above)
2 cans apricot halves in syrup
1 cup heavy cream

1. Make two jelly roll sponges but do not spread with jelly or roll up.

2. Cut out circles of sponge, 2–2½ inches in diameter.

3. Place an apricot half on each sponge circle. Whip the cream until stiff and pipe rosettes of cream around each apricot half. If the cakes are not going to be eaten straight away, coat the apricots in sugar syrup, dissolved unflavored gelatin, or melted apricot jam and refrigerate until serving.

If you have children, you need not worry about the leftover scraps of jelly roll sponge going to waste. When baking a fat-free sponge, ensure that it is not in the oven for too long, otherwise the sponge becomes fragile and breaks easily.

Jelly Roll Gateau
(Rouladentorte)

For the fat-free sponge:
6 egg yolks, ½ cup superfine granulated sugar
6 egg whites, 7 teaspoons all-purpose flour
7 teaspoons cornstarch, 1 jar orange marmalade
For the orange custard:
1 envelope unflavored gelatin, 3 egg yolks,
10 tablespoons superfine granulated sugar, Juice of 1 lemon
1½ cups orange juice, 6 egg whites, stiffly beaten
Extra:
½ cup confectioners' sugar, 2–3 tablespoons orange juice

1. <u>For the sponge:</u> Preheat the oven to 350°F. Make a jelly roll sponge according to the Jelly Roll recipe on page 128.

2. Turn the baked sponge out onto a damp dish cloth and allow to cool. Carefully remove the baking parchment. Spread the orange marmalade over the sponge to the thickness you prefer. Using the dish cloth to help you, starting from a short side, roll up the sponge.

3. Cut the sponge into one-inch thick slices. Line a springform pan with baking parchment. Arrange the slices of jelly roll close together in the pan, laying them on their sides.

4. <u>For the orange custard:</u> Dissolve the unflavored gelatin in a little hot water. Whisk the egg yolks and the sugar together until frothy. Add the lemon juice and orange juice. Carefully fold in the unflavored gelatin. Finally fold in the egg whites. Refrigerate the custard for 1 hour.

5. Fill any gaps in the layer of sponge cake with the orange custard. Refrigerate the gateau overnight, so it sets.

6. Turn out the gateau onto a plate. Mix the confectioners' sugar with the orange juice to make a thick glaze, and pour it over the gateau. It may be necessary to adjust the quantities of sugar and juice depending on the thickness of glaze required.

On warm summer days this gateau is a very good dessert for a cold buffet.

Carrot Cake
(Gelbe Rübentorte)

8 egg yolks
1 cup + 3½ tablespoons superfine granulated sugar
1 pound carrots, peeled and finely grated
1¼ cups ground almonds
3 tablespoons cornstarch
3 tablespoons rum
1 tablespoon ground cinnamon
6 egg whites, stiffly beaten
Butter and dry breadcrumbs for the pan
3–4 tablespoons apricot jelly
2 tablespoons apricot schnapps
¼ pound semi-sweet cooking chocolate

1. Preheat the oven to 350°F. Whisk the egg yolks and sugar together until very frothy. Gradually add the carrots, almonds, cornstarch, rum, and cinnamon, and mix well. Finally, lightly fold in the beaten egg whites.

2. Butter a 10-inch springform pan and dust it with the breadcrumbs. Pour the cake mixture into the buttered pan and bake on the middle oven shelf for about 1 hour until golden brown.

3. Turn the cake out and allow to cool on a wire rack. Put the apricot jelly in a saucepan with the apricot schnapps. Warm through and brush the glaze all over the cooled cake. Break the chocolate into pieces and put it in a bowl over a saucepan of barely simmering water. Melt the chocolate slowly over low heat. Coat the glazed cake in the melted chocolate.

It is worth baking the cake two days before you intend to serve it, because that way the flavor develops fully.

Chocolate Cranberry Torte
(Wachauertorte)

For the cake:
7 egg yolks
10 tablespoons superfine granulated sugar
10 tablespoons ground almonds
3 level tablespoons cocoa powder
7 egg whites, stiffly beaten
Butter and dry breadcrumbs for the pan
For the cream filling:
½ cup butter, softened, ½ cup confectioners' sugar
1 small egg, beaten
2 tablespoons cocoa powder, 5 tablespoons rum
About 1 pound cranberry preserve

1. For the cake: Preheat the oven to 350°F. Whisk the egg yolks and sugar together until very frothy. Add the ground almonds and cocoa, and mix well. Carefully fold in the beaten egg whites. Butter a springform pan, and dust it with the breadcrumbs. Bake the cake until risen and golden brown. Allow it to cool overnight.

2. For the cream filling: Beat the butter and confectioners' sugar together until creamy. Add the beaten egg, cocoa, and 2 tablespoons of the rum. Mix all the ingredients together thoroughly.

3. Slice the cake into two layers. Drizzle half the remaining rum over the bottom layer. Spread all the cranberry preserves over it, followed by two-thirds of the chocolate cream. Sandwich the second layer of sponge on top. Prick it all over with a fork. Drizzle the remaining rum over the top of the cake, and spread with the remaining chocolate cream. Refrigerate overnight.

Coffee Cream Gateau
(Biskuithaufen)

1 cup butter
13 tablespoons superfine granulated sugar
2 eggs, beaten
2 tablespoons instant coffee
Lady fingers (1–2 packages)
4–5 tablespoons rum
4–5 tablespoons cranberry preserves
Chocolate-coated coffee beans to garnish

1. Beat the butter and sugar together until light and fluffy. Gradually add the beaten eggs. Dissolve the instant coffee in a splash of hot water. Allow the coffee to cool, then beat it, drop by drop, into the butter mixture.

2. Line the bottom of a 9-inch springform pan with ladyfingers. Drizzle a little rum over them. Spread them first with a layer of cranberry preserves, then with a layer of coffee cream. Cover the filling with another layer of sponge fingers. Continue layering the ladyfingers and filling, finishing with a layer of ladyfingers. There should be a quantity of coffee cream left over. Refrigerate the cake and the remaining coffee cream overnight.

3. Release the sides of the springform pan. Put the gateau on a cake plate and spread with the remaining coffee cream. Garnish the gateau with chocolate-covered coffee beans. Refrigerate before serving.

Instead of the chocolate-covered coffee beans, you can garnish the gateau with rosettes of whipped cream.

Aviva's Chocolate Cake
(Avivas Schokoladentorte)

Generous ¾ stick butter, softened
10 tablespoons superfine granulated sugar
6 egg yolks
½ pound bitter-sweet chocolate
6 egg whites, stiffly beaten
Butter and dry breadcrumbs for the cake pan

1. Preheat the oven to 350°F. Beat together the softened butter, sugar, and egg yolks until frothy. Break the chocolate into pieces, put it in a bowl over a saucepan of barely simmering water, and melt it. Slowly stir it into the egg mixture. Fold the stiffly beaten egg whites lightly into the chocolate mixture.

2. Reserve 3–4 tablespoons of the cake mixture, and refrigerate.

3. Butter a cake pan, and dust it with the breadcrumbs. Pour the cake mixture into the pan and smooth the top. Bake the cake on the middle oven shelf for about 40 minutes.

4. Allow the cake to cool, turn it out of the pan, and place it on a cake plate. Spread the reserved, uncooked cake mixture over the cake.

Even if the cake sinks a little as it cools, it doesn't spoil the superb taste.

Spice Cake
(Gewürzkuchen)

<u>Version I:</u>
1 cup butter, softened, 1 cup superfine granulated sugar
8 egg yolks, beaten, ½ cup chocolate, melted
1 teaspoon ground cinnamon, ¼ teaspoon ground cloves
½ cup diced candied orange and lemon peel, 1 cup ground hazelnuts
3½ tablespoons dry breadcrumbs, ½ teaspoon baking powder
6 egg whites, stiffly beaten
<u>Version II:</u>
½ cup butter, softened, 1 cup + 3½ tablespoons superfine granulated sugar
4–5 egg yolks, beaten, ½ cup semi-sweet chocolate, melted
1 teaspoon ground cinnamon, ¼ teaspoon ground cloves
½ teaspoon grated nutmeg, ¾ cup heavy cream
1⅓ cups all-purpose flour, 2 teaspoons baking powder
4–5 egg whites, stiffly beaten

1. Both cakes are prepared in the same way. Preheat the oven to 350°F.

2. Beat the butter and sugar until creamy. Gradually add the egg yolks and beat until light and frothy.

3. Gradually fold in the chocolate, cinnamon, cloves, candied peel or nutmeg, ground nuts or cream, breadcrumbs or flour, and baking powder. Finally fold in the stiffly beaten egg whites.

4. Butter a 10-inch springform pan and dust it with breadcrumbs. Transfer the cake mixture to the pan and bake the cake on the middle oven shelf for about 1 hour.

5. Take the cake out of the oven and allow it to cool in the pan. Turn it out of the pan and put it on a cake plate. The cooled cake can be coated with a sugar frosting, flavored with rum and decorated with little chocolate leaves. Alternatively, you can pipe circles of chocolate onto the cake, and draw a toothpick through them, to create a feathered pattern.

Madeira Cake
(Sandkuchen)

1 cup butter, softened
1 cup superfine granulated sugar
6 eggs, beaten
1½ cups cornstarch
½ cup all-purpose flour
1 teaspoon baking powder
1 tablespoon rum
Butter and dry breadcrumbs for the pans
10 tablespoons confectioners' sugar
1 tablespoon cocoa powder
1–2 tablespoons hot water
½ tablespoon butter, melted

1. Preheat the oven to 350°F. Beat the butter and sugar together until light and creamy. Gradually add the eggs. Sift together the cornstarch, flour, and baking powder. Add the flour to the egg mixture, then add the rum. Beat the cake mixture for 5–10 minutes with a hand-held electric mixer.

2. Butter two medium-size loaf pans, and dust them with breadcrumbs. Transfer the cake mixture to the pans and smooth the top of the mixture. Bake the cakes on the middle oven shelf for 45 minutes.

3. Blend the confectioners' sugar, cocoa powder, and hot water together. Add the melted butter, drop by drop, and stir it into the icing. Turn the cakes out of the pans, and coat the hot cakes with the chocolate icing.

If you wrap the cold cakes in foil, they will keep in the refrigerator for at least two weeks.

Sponge Cake
(Kastenkuchen)

1 stick + 1 tablespoon butter
9 tablespoons superfine granulated sugar
2 eggs
9 tablespoons all-purpose flour
1 tablespoon rum
Butter and dry breadcrumbs for the pan

1. Preheat the oven to 350°F. Beat the butter and sugar together until light and fluffy. Gradually add the eggs and beat in the flour and rum.

2. Butter a loaf pan, and dust it with the breadcrumbs. Transfer the mixture to the pan and smooth the top. Bake on the middle oven shelf for about 30 minutes until golden brown.

This cake mixture is also very suitable as a base for a fruit topping, such as apples, or cherries.
Because the recipe uses equal quantities of butter, sugar, and flour for each egg, you can increase the quantity of cake mixture to suit.

Chestnut Cake
(Kastanienkuchen)

1 pound chestnuts, 2 cups milk
1¼ sticks butter, softened
¾ cup superfine granulated sugar,
6 egg yolks, beaten
½ teaspoon vanilla extract
¼ cup ground almonds
6 egg whites, stiffly beaten
Butter and dry breadcrumbs for the pan
10 tablespoons confectioners' sugar
1 tablespoon cocoa powder
1–2 tablespoons hot water
½ tablespoon butter, melted

1. Preheat the oven to 425°F. Score a cross on each chestnut. Put the chestnuts on a baking sheet and bake them in the hot oven until the shells start to peel back. Allow them to cool, then peel them. Put the chestnuts in a saucepan with the milk. Bring to a boil and simmer until the chestnuts are soft. Drain the chestnuts, reserving the milk, and purée in a blender.

2. Reduce the oven temperature to 350°F. Beat the butter and sugar together until light and fluffy, then add the egg yolks and vanilla extract. Fold the chestnut purée, ground almonds, and a cup of the reserved chestnut milk into the egg mixture. Fold in the stiffly beaten egg whites.

3. Butter a 10-inch springform pan and dust it with the breadcrumbs. Spoon the cake mixture into the pan and bake it for 1 hour.

4. When the cake has cooled, coat it with chocolate frosting made according to the directions for Madeira Cake page 134.

Fruit Bread
(Früchtebrot)

1 cup raisins
½ cup currants
5 tablespoons kirsch
4 eggs
1 cup superfine granulated sugar
¼ cup semi-sweet chocolate, coarsely chopped
½ cup candied orange and lemon peel
½ cup whole almonds
1 teaspoon ground cinnamon
½ teaspoon ground cloves
1 cup all-purpose flour
Butter and dry breadcrumbs for the pan

1. Put the raisins and currants in a bowl and pour the kirsch over them. Marinate the fruit for at least 30 minutes. Preheat the oven to 350°F.

2. Beat the eggs and sugar together until very frothy. Gradually stir in the chopped chocolate, marinated currants and raisins, candied peel, whole almonds, cinnamon, and cloves. Finally fold in the flour.

3. Butter a loaf pan and dust it with the breadcrumbs. Transfer the cake mixture to the pan and bake it for 1–1¼ hours.

The fruit bread should be baked two to three weeks before serving, so the flavor can develop fully. Because the quantity of cake mixture is enough to fill a 3½ cup loaf pan, I prepare a double quantity and use it to fill three medium-size pans.

Cheesecake
(Käsekuchen)

For the pastry:
¾ stick + ½ tablespoon butter, 13 tablespoons all-purpose flour
2 pinches of baking powder
6½ tablespoons superfine granulated sugar, 2 eggs, beaten
For the topping:
½ cup butter, 7 tablespoons superfine granulated sugar
4 teaspoons vanilla sugar, 4 egg yolks
2 cups low fat ricotta or cottage cheese, 1 cup cream cheese
¼ cup cornstarch + ½ teaspoon vanilla extract, 1 cup heavy cream, stiffly whipped
Butter and dry breadcrumbs for the pan
For the meringue:
4 egg whites, 8 level tablespoons superfine granulated sugar

1. For the pastry: Sift the flour and baking powder into a bowl. Rub the butter into the flour, until the texture resembles fine breadcrumbs. Stir the sugar into the flour mixture, then mix in the beaten eggs. Work the mixture together quickly to form a dough, wrap it in plastic wrap, and chill in the refrigerator for at least 30 minutes.

2. For the topping: Beat the butter, sugar, vanilla sugar, and egg yolks together until light and fluffy. Stir in the ricotta cheese, cream cheese, cornstarch, and vanilla extract. Finally fold in the stiffly whipped cream.

3. Butter a 10–inch springform pan, and dust it with the breadcrumbs. Line the bottom and sides of the pan with the shortcrust pastry. Fill the pastry case with the cheese filling. Put the pan into a cold oven, heat the oven to 350°F, and bake the cheesecake until the pastry is golden brown.

4. For the meringue: Beat the egg whites until stiff, gradually adding the sugar in a slow trickle. Continue beating until the meringue stands in firm peaks and is very glossy. Spread the meringue over the cheesecake, and bake it for a further 15 minutes.

It is advisable to cover the cheesecake and leave it to cool in the pan for 24 hours.

Rich Shortcrust Pastry Fruit Tarts

(Gerührter Mürbeteig für Obstkuchen)

For the pastry:
1 cup + 2 tablespoons butter, softened
½ cup superfine granulated sugar
4 egg yolks, beaten
1 cup + 2 tablespoons all-purpose flour
Juice of ½ lemon
2 pinches ground cinnamon
Butter and dry breadcrumbs for the pan
For the meringue:
4 egg whites
6½ tablespoons superfine granulated sugar
½ cup ground almonds
For the filling:
2 pounds red currants, or any other fresh, seasonal fruit

1. For the pastry: Preheat the oven to 350°F. Beat the butter and sugar together until light and fluffy. Gradually beat in the egg yolks, flour, lemon juice, and cinnamon. Work the ingredients together quickly to form a dough. Wrap the pastry in plastic wrap and chill it in the refrigerator for at least 30 minutes.

2. Butter the two springform pans and sprinkle with the breadcrumbs. Fill the pastry cases with dried beans or pie weights, and blind bake until golden brown.

3. For the meringue: Beat the egg whites until very stiff, adding the sugar in a slow trickle. Continue beating until the meringue stands in firm peaks and is very glossy. Sprinkle the ground almonds over the meringue,and carefully fold them in.

4. Allow the pastry cases to cool. Wash and drain the red currents. Cover the pastry cases with the prepared fruit. Spread an even layer of meringue over each of the pies. Put the meringue-topped pies in the oven at maximum heat for a short time, until the meringue is dry.

I prefer using lightweight foil pie plates for baking these pastry cases, so I can freeze the pastry case later. This way, I always have a pastry case available to fill with the appropriate fruits of the season. Fresh redcurrants are a delicious, refreshing filling in summer; in winter I often use peaches or apricots in syrup, and top them with meringue, too. If you haven't time to make the meringue, you can always garnish the tart with whipped cream.

Nut Ring
(Nußkranz)

For the yeast dough:
2 cups all-purpose flour, 2 ounces cake yeast
crumbled, or dry yeast (check yeast-to-flour ratio on packet)
6½ tablespoons sugar, 1 cup lukewarm milk
2 eggs, beaten, Pinch of salt to taste
For the filling:
1 cup milk, 1–2 tablespoons honey
8 teaspoons butter, 13 tablespoons sugar
1 cup + 3½ tablespoons ground hazelnuts or almonds, 6½ tablespoons fresh breadcrumbs
Butter and breadcrumbs for the ring mold, 1 cup raisins
½ stick butter, melted, Confectioners' sugar for dusting

1. For the yeast dough: Sift the flour into a bowl. Make a well in the center. Put the crumbled yeast in the well with a teaspoon of the sugar and a splash of the lukewarm milk. Mix them together lightly, incorporating a little of the flour from the sides of the well. Sprinkle a pinch of flour over the yeast mixture, and leave it in a warm place for 30 minutes.

2. Combine the yeast mixture and flour with the remaining sugar, eggs, salt, and the remaining milk to form a stiff dough. Beat hard with a wooden spoon until air bubbles appear in it. Leave to rise again for 30 minutes.

3. For the filling: Put the milk, honey, butter, and sugar in a saucepan, and bring to a boil. Stir in the hazelnuts or almonds, and the breadcrumbs.

4. If the mixture is too stiff, add a splash of water. It should have a spreadable, porridge-like consistency.

5. Preheat the oven to 400°F. Butter a ring mold and dust it with breadcrumbs. Roll out the dough. Spread the nut mixture over the dough and sprinkle over the raisins, then roll it up to form a sausage. Shape it into a semicircle and place in the ring mold. Bake the nut ring until golden brown.

6. When the cake has cooled, turn it out of the ring mold. Brush with melted butter and dust with the confectioners' sugar.

Great-Grandmother's Yeast Cake
(Urgroßmutters gerührter Bund)

1 cup clarified butter
½ cup superfine granulated sugar
2 cups all-purpose flour
8 eggs
Grated zest of 1 lemon
1 cup sour cream
1½ ounces fresh yeast, or dry yeast (check yeast-to-flour ratio on packet)
1 cup lukewarm milk
Butter for the mold
3–4 tablespoons flaked or chopped almonds

1. Beat the clarified butter and sugar together until light and fluffy. First beat in one tablespoon of flour, then one egg, the zest of lemon, and one tablespoon of sour cream. Continue in this way until the ingredients are used up.

2. Dissolve the yeast in the lukewarm milk, and add to the mixture. Beat until air bubbles form.

3. Butter a ring mold and dust it with the flaked or chopped almonds. Carefully pour the batter into the mold and level the top.

4. Put the mold in a cold oven. Heat the oven to 100°F, and leave the batter to rise for 30 minutes. The batter should rise by a depth of two fingers.

5. Increase the oven temperature to 350°F, and bake for about 1 hour, until golden brown. Cover the cake and leave it to cool in the mold, then turn it out onto a cake plate.

Screwdrivers
(Schraubenzieher)

1 cup all-purpose flour
¾ ounce fresh yeast, or dry yeast (check yeast-to-flour ratio on packet)
Splash of lukewarm milk
Pinch of salt to taste
½ cup butter, chilled and diced
3½ tablespoons granulated sugar
1 egg, beaten
½ cup + 2 tablespoons coarse-grained sugar
Butter for the baking sheet

1. Sift the flour onto a work surface. Dissolve the yeast in the milk. Add the salt, diced butter, granulated sugar, egg, and yeast to the flour, and knead all the ingredients together to form a stiff dough. Transfer the dough to a bowl, cover, and leave it to rise in a warm place.

2. Knead the dough briefly. It should be easy to roll out. If it is too soft, add a little more flour. Sprinkle the candy sugar over the work surface. Roll the dough into several 4-inch-long strips. Wrap parts of strips around each other to form twists.

3. Butter the baking sheet. Place the twists on the baking sheet, cover, and leave to rise again. Preheat the oven to 350°F. Bake the screwdrivers until golden brown.

For a change, you can use sesame seeds instead of the candy sugar. If you store the pastries in an airtight container, they will stay fresh for several days. This dough is also suitable for all kinds of fruit pastries.

Apple and Cottage Cheese Strudel
(Apfel- und Quarkstrudel)

<u>For the strudel dough:</u>
I cup milk, ½ stick + I tablespoon butter
Sugar to taste, 4 cups all-purpose flour
Pinch of salt to taste, I egg, beaten
<u>For the apple filling:</u>
2 pounds ripe cooking apples, I cup sour cream or
I ½ sticks + I tablespoon butter, melted, Sugar and ground cinnamon to taste
I cup milk, ½ cup butter, melted, for brushing
<u>For the cheese filling:</u>
3 cups low fat cottage cheese, 2 eggs, beaten
4 tablespoons superfine granulated sugar, Pinch of salt to taste
Scant cup of heavy cream, 2 handfuls sultanas, rinsed

1. <u>For the dough:</u> put the milk, butter, and sugar in a saucepan. Bring to a boil and set aside.

2. Sift the flour with a pinch of salt onto a work surface. Make a well in the center. Add the egg and cooled milk. Using a fork, combine the egg, milk, and flour. When the flour is incorporated, start to knead the dough with your hands, and continue kneading until pockets of air form in the dough. Divide the dough into four portions, transfer it to a plate or bowl, cover, and leave in a warm place for an hour, to rise.

3. Roll out each portion of the strudel dough on a damp cloth. Carefully stretch the dough over your knuckles, taking care not to tear it, until the dough is very thin, almost translucent.

4. <u>For the filling:</u> peel and core the apples. Slice them thin. Brush the strudel dough with the sour cream or melted butter. Cover each piece of dough with a layer of sliced apples. Sprinkle the sugar and cinnamon on top. Using the cloth to help you, roll up the strudel.

5. Preheat the oven to 400°F. Butter a rectangular, ovenproof dish and place the strudels in it. Baste them with the milk and brush them with the melted butter. Bake for 45 minutes, occasionally basting with milk and brushing with butter until golden brown.

6. The strudel also tastes delicious with a cottage cheese filling: Blend together the cottage cheese, eggs, sugar, salt, and cream to form a smooth paste. Brush the strudel pastry with melted butter, then spread the cheese mixture over the pastry. Sprinkle the raisins over the cheese filling, roll up the strudels, and bake them in the same way as the apple strudels.

I prefer the dough described above for sweet strudels. For savory strudels,
I make the dough with 1 cup bread flour, 1 egg, 2 teaspoons oil,
a pinch of salt to taste, and ½ cup of lukewarm water.
The method is the same as described above.

Snowballs
(Schneeballen)

2 eggs
2 egg yolks
8 teaspoons butter, softened
Pinch of salt to taste
4 tablespoons heavy cream
1–4 tablespoons sugar, to taste
2 cups all-purpose flour
Corn oil for deep frying
Confectioners' sugar for dusting

1. Beat the eggs, egg yolks, butter, salt, cream, and sugar together. Work the flour into the egg mixture, and knead it until a smooth dough forms.

2. Break off small portions from the dough, and roll them out to form thin discs. Place the pastry circles between two dish towels, and allow them to dry out a little.

3. Using a pastry wheel or a knife, make cuts in the pastry, but leave an uncut border all around. Heat the oil to 350°F in a deep-fat fryer or a deep saucepan.

4. Thread the handle of a wooden spoon through the slits in the pastry. Dip the handle of the spoon into the hot oil and hold it there until the pastry is cooked. As the pastry cooks, it should curl up into a bowl. Help bring the pastry circles into shape using two forks. Drain the pastries and dust them with confectioners' sugar.

The "snowballs" will keep for up to three weeks if stored in an airtight container. Dust them with confectioners' sugar just before serving them.

Almond Peaks
(Mandelmutzen)

1¼ sticks butter, softened
½ cup superfine granulated sugar
3 eggs, beaten
2–3 drops bitter almond oil
2 tablespoons rum
2 cups all-purpose flour
2 teaspoons baking powder
Corn oil for deep frying
Sugar for sprinkling

1. Beat the butter and sugar together using a hand-held electric mixer until light and fluffy. Gradually beat in the eggs, almond oil, and rum.

2. Mix together the flour and baking powder. Sift the flour onto the egg mixture and quickly stir it in.

3. Heat the oil to 350°F in a deep-fat fryer or deep saucepan.

4. Using a teaspoon, scoop off small, peaked portions of dough and drop them into the hot oil. Fry batches of the almond peaks until golden brown.

5. Remove the almond peaks from the hot oil using a skimmer and drain them on paper towels. When they have cooled, sprinkle them with sugar.

This is a typical Rhineland treat for Shrove Tuesday. If you like, you can mix the sugar for sprinkling with fresh vanilla extract, or ground cinnamon.

Grandmother Merz's Butter Cookies

(Butterzeug nach Großmutter Merz)

1 cup + 2 tablespoons clarified butter, softened
1 cup + 2 tablespoons superfine granulated sugar
4 egg yolks, beaten
2½ cups all-purpose flour
Grated zest of 1 lemon
2 tablespoons rum
1 teaspoon ground cinnamon
5 tablespoons granulated sugar

1. Beat the butter until light and fluffy. Gradually add all the remaining ingredients (except for the ground cinnamon and 5 table-spoons of sugar) and work the mixture until a smooth dough forms. Cover the dough and allow it to rest.

2. Preheat the oven to 350°F.

3. Roll the dough out thin on a floured work surface. Cut out shapes with cookie cutters. Line a baking sheet with baking parchment. Place the cookies on the baking sheet and bake for about 15 minutes until golden brown.

4. Mix the sugar and cinnamon together. Using a spatula, carefully lift the cookies off the baking sheet and dredge them in the cinnamon sugar. Allow the cookies to cool, then store them in an airtight container.

The butter cookies only develop their full flavor a few days after baking.

Vanilla Slices

(Vanilleschnitten)

For the pastry:
1½ cups all-purpose flour
1 cup butter, softened
6½ tablespoons superfine granulated sugar
2 tablespoons sour cream
For the topping:
4 egg whites
1 cup confectioners' sugar
1 cup ground almonds
2 teaspoons vanilla sugar

For the pastry:
1. Sift the flour into a bowl. Rub the butter into the flour until it resembles fine bread-crumbs. Stir the sugar and sour cream into the flour and knead the mixture to form a smooth dough.

2. Roll out the dough on a floured work surface to about ¼–inch thick. Cut it into finger-length strips. Allow to rest in the refrigerator overnight.

For the topping:
3. Beat the egg whites, gradually adding the confectioners' sugar, until they stand in stiff peaks and are very glossy. Fold the almonds and vanilla sugar into the meringue mixture.

4. Preheat the oven to 350°F. Carefully spread the meringue over the pastry fingers. Bake until pale golden brown.

It's a good idea to use two small spoons to spread the meringue over the pastry fingers, leaving a pastry border around the edge of each slice.

Almond Rings
(Mandelkränzchen)

1½ cups all-purpose flour
1 cup butter, softened
½ cup superfine granulated sugar
2 pinches ground cloves
1 teaspoon ground cinnamon
1 cup ground almonds
2 eggs, beaten
Vanilla sugar for sprinkling

1. Sift the flour into a bowl. Rub the butter into the flour until the mixture resembles fine breadcrumbs. Stir the sugar, cloves, cinnamon, and almonds into the mixture. Add the beaten eggs and knead to form a smooth dough. Allow the dough to rest for 1 hour in the refrigerator.

2. Preheat the oven to 350°F. Roll the dough out thin on a floured work surface. Using a medium-size cookie cutter, cut out circles from the dough. Cut a smaller circle out of the cookies with another cutter, to make rings. Reroll the smaller cuttings and repeat this procedure until the whole dough is used. Brush the rings with water, and sprinkle the vanilla sugar over them.

3. Line a baking sheet with baking parchment. Place the cookies on the sheet and bake for about 15 minutes, or until golden brown.

Instead of sprinkling the cookies with sugar, you can coat them with frosting after baking and sprinkle them with chopped almonds or chopped pistachio nuts.

Jammy Dodgers
(Türkische Mundbissen)

See the Almond Ring recipe opposite for ingredients and quantities.

Filling:
1½ cups raspberry preserves
For the cinnamon icing:
4 tablespoons white wine
2 tablespoons confectioners' sugar
4 pinches ground cinnamon

1. Prepare the dough as described for Almond Rings.

2. Roll the dough out thin on a floured work surface. Cut out circles from the dough. With another cutter, cut a smaller circle out of half of the cookies to make rings. Cover the cookies and allow them to rest overnight at room temperature.

3. Preheat the oven to 350°F. Line a baking sheet with baking parchment. Place the cookies and rings on the sheet and bake for 10–15 minutes, or until pale golden brown.

4. When the cookies have cooled a little, spread the solid cookies with raspberry preserve and place a ring cookie on top of each.

5. Blend the white wine, confectioners' sugar, and cinnamon together to form a smooth paste and spread the frosting over the rings.

Almond Macaroons
(Mandelmakronen)

4 egg whites
13 tablespoons superfine granulated sugar
1¼ cups ground almonds
Approximately 40 parchment paper circles,
2 inches in diameter

1. Beat the egg whites, adding the sugar in a slow trickle, until glossy and standing in stiff peaks. Carefully fold the ground almonds into the meringue.

2. Preheat the oven to 300°F.

3. Place the circles of parchment paper on a baking sheet. Using 2 teaspoons, pile portions of almond meringue mixture onto them.

4. Bake the macaroons very slowly in the oven, so they dry out. The macaroons should not brown at all.

If you mix roasted, finely ground hazelnuts into the meringue, you will have hazelnut macaroons. You can also use toasted, dried coconut. After baking the macaroons can also be placed upside down on wax paper, and the bases coated with melted chocolate.

Elisenlebkuchen
(Elisenlebkuchen)

2 eggs
13 tablespoons superfine granulated sugar
2 teaspoons vanilla sugar
Pinch of ground cloves
1 teaspoon ground cinnamon
Splash of rum
½ cup finely chopped candied orange and lemon peel
½ cup ground almonds
5 tablespoons ground hazelnuts
Approximately 40 parchment paper circles, 3 inches in diameter
For the pale frosting:
10 tablespoons confectioners' sugar
2 tablespoons rum
For the dark frosting:
6½ tablespoons confectioners' sugar
1 tablespoon cocoa powder
1–2 tablespoons hot water
½ tablespoon melted butter

1. Beat the eggs and superfine sugar together until thick and creamy. Gradually fold in the vanilla sugar, cloves, cinnamon, rum, candied peel, almonds, and hazelnuts.

2. Preheat the oven to 300°F. Divide the mixture equally among the parchment paper circles. Smooth them off using a damp knife. Bake the *lebkuchen* for 25–35 minutes.

3. To make the frostings, blend the ingredients together to form a smooth, glossy paste. Coat half of the *lebkuchen* in the pale frosting and half in the dark.

Great-Grandmother Rosenhauer's Christmas Cake
(Christstollen nach Urgroßmutter Rosenhauer)

5½ pounds all-purpose flour, ¼ pound fresh cake yeast
crumbled, or dry yeast (check yeast-to-flour ration on packet)
1 cup superfine granulated sugar, 4 cups lukewarm milk
3 eggs, beaten, Pinch of salt to taste
2½ cups butter, softened, 2 cups raisins
Zest of 1 lemon, 1 cup candied orange and lemon peel
13 tablespoons slivered almonds, 3–4 tablespoons rum
1 cup butter, melted, Confectioners' sugar for dusting

1. Sift the flour into a bowl. Make a well in the center. Put the yeast in the well with a teaspoon of the sugar and a splash of the lukewarm milk. Work some of the flour from the edge of the well into the yeast and milk, then sprinkle a pinch of flour on top of the yeast mixture and leave it for 30 minutes in a warm place.

2. Work the remaining sugar, the eggs, salt, and remaining milk into the yeast mixture to form a stiff batter. Beat the batter with a wooden spoon until pockets of air form. Add the butter, raisins, lemon zest, candied peel, almonds, and rum to the batter and work them in.

3. Cover the dough and leave it to rise in a warm place for at least an hour.

4. Preheat the oven to 350°F. Knead the dough again, and divide it into five portions.

5. Shape each portion of dough into a longish, flattish oval, then fold it in half. Leave it to rise in a warm place again.

6. Bake the *stollen* on a baking sheet for 40–45 minutes.

7. Remove from the oven and brush immediately with some of the melted butter. Sift lots of confectioners' sugar onto the *stollen*. Wrap them in foil and allow them to cool, then refrigerate.

8. Next day, unwrap the cakes. Brush them with more melted butter and dust thickly with confectioners' sugar again. Repeat this process, then wrap the cakes in foil again, and store in a cool place until required.

The stollen *will be especially light if the butter that is added to the dough is first beaten until light and fluffy. The* stollen *gets its typical Christmassy shine from the repeated coating with butter and confectioners' sugar. This thick sugar coating also prevents the cake from drying out.*

*I*n the past, a household without a larder was almost unthinkable, but of course in those days houses still had large cellars or storerooms. Nowadays the options for building up a store of food are usually reduced to a refrigerator and how much it can hold. Because of central heating, cellars are usually too warm, making long-term storage virtually impossible.

In any case, the need to build up supplies is no longer so great, because you can get almost everything fresh all year round and very few people live far from the nearest supermarket. Yet there is the urge to hoard provisions, like a squirrel, in all of us, and we all wax nostalgic over grandmother's homemade pumpkin pickle, Auntie Julia's sweet-and-sour pears, or the unforgettable advocaat that, as children, we loved to lick from our parents' almost empty glasses. A jar of homemade mustard, fruit preserved in rum, or preserved garlic is always welcome as a gift.

Mild Mustard
(Süßer Senf)

1 cup water
4 cups white wine vinegar
1 pound sugar
2 bay leaves
6 peppercorns
3 cloves
8 juniper berries
1 onion, peeled and sliced
1 cup ground yellow mustard seeds
½ cup ground green mustard seeds

1. Put the water, vinegar, sugar, bay leaves, peppercorns, cloves, juniper berries, and onion in a saucepan, bring to a boil, and boil for at least 20 minutes.

2. Put the ground mustard seeds in a large bowl. Strain the liquid through a sieve onto the ground seeds and mix thoroughly.

3. Transfer the mustard to prepared jars, cover tightly, and allow to rest for at least 3–4 weeks.

Impatience won't be rewarded, because mustard that is not allowed to mature tastes bitter. If the paste is too thick, dilute it with sugar syrup.

Tomato Ketchup
(Tomatenketchup)

12 pounds very ripe tomatoes
1 pound red bell peppers
3 large onions
2 cups red wine vinegar
2 cups red wine
3 tablespoons salt
3 tablespoons freshly grated horseradish
Pinch of ground cloves
Pinch of cayenne pepper
1¼ cup tablespoons sugar

1. Wash and quarter the tomatoes. Halve, core, seed, and chop the peppers. Peel and roughly chop the onions. Purée together the tomatoes, peppers, and onions. Put the purée in a saucepan, bring to a boil, and simmer for 30 minutes, stirring occasionally.

2. Push the tomato mixture through a sieve into a clean, large saucepan. Stir in the vinegar, red wine, salt, horseradish, cloves, and cayenne. Bring to a boil and simmer uncovered, over a low heat, for 2–4 hours.

3. As soon as the ketchup has reduced and thickened, add the sugar, mix well, and simmer for a few minutes longer.

4. Pour the hot ketchup into prepared jars and close tightly.

Pickled Cabbage
(Einlegen von Sauerkraut)

2 pounds white cabbage
6½ tablespoons salt
Juniper berries to taste
Peppercorns and bay leaves to taste

1. Cut the cabbages in half, remove the cores, and grate the cabbage fine.

2. Layer the grated cabbage in a stone crock with the salt, juniper berries, peppercorns, and bay leaves, pressing each layer down well. Each layer of cabbage should run juice. Continue until the final layer of cabbage comes just below the rim of the crock.

3. Cover the cabbage with a linen cloth. Put a saucer or plate that just fits inside the crock on top and weigh it down. The cabbage juice should rise over the saucer. If it doesn't, the cabbage is too dry, and you should add a little weak brine to the crock. Close the crock tightly. The more the cabbage is weighted, and the tighter the seal, the better the finished cabbage will taste.

4. Store for about 6 weeks at room temperature. Rinse the saucer with cold water occasionally, and rinse out the linen cloth, so the cabbage remains fresh and edible.

Our son and daughter-in-law have been pickling cabbage for years, and it's the best I've ever had. Maybe it has something to do with the skill of our grandchildren, Maximilian and Constanze, at stamping down the cabbage.

Preserved Garlic
(Eingelegter Knoblauch)

1 cup white wine
1 cup vinegar
5 tablespoons sugar
2 teaspoons salt
2 chili peppers
1 sprig rosemary
1 sprig thyme
8 cloves
1 teaspoon peppercorns
4 bay leaves
10 very fresh whole garlic bulbs
4–6 tablespoons olive oil

1. Put the wine, vinegar, sugar, salt, chiles, rosemary, thyme, cloves, peppercorns, and bay leaves in a saucepan, bring to a boil, and simmer gently for a few minutes.

2. Separate the cloves of garlic, peel them, and add them to the liquid. Bring to a boil again, and simmer the garlic for 3 minutes, then take off the heat, and allow to cool.

3. Remove the cloves of garlic from the liquid and put them in prepared jars. Bring the liquid to a boil again and pour the hot liquid over the garlic. Allow to cool, then finally top up each jar with a splash of olive oil and close tightly.

Preserved Walnuts
(Eingelegte Walnüsse)

50 walnuts
5 cups + 6½ tablespoons sugar
Cloves to taste
1 cinnamon stick, chopped
Sugar syrup see below

1. Pick nice, large green walnuts. Prick the soft shuck 4–8 times with a large needle, then soak the nuts in water for 9 days, changing the water daily.

2. Bring a saucepan of water to a boil, add the drained nuts, and bring to a boil 2 or 3 times. Remove the walnuts and drain in a colander.

3. Spike the walnuts with cloves and pieces of cinnamon stick. Put them in prepared jars and pour the sugar syrup over them. Place a saucer on top of the walnuts and weigh it down, so that the walnuts are competely immersed in the syrup. Leave in a cool place to rest for several days.

4. Strain the sugar syrup into a saucepan. Add some more sugar, bring to a boil, and allow them to cool. Pour the cold sugar syrup over the nuts and allow to rest for several days.

5. Put the syrup and nuts in a saucepan, bring to a boil, and simmer until soft. Transfer the nuts and syrup to prepared jars and close tightly.

To make the sugar syrup, boil equal quantities of water and sugar until, if you dip a fork in the syrup, threads form when you pull the fork away.

Sweet-and-Sour Pears
(Birnen süß-sauer)

7 pounds pears
6 cups wine vinegar
4 cups sugar
Grated zest of 1 lemon
1 cinnamon stick
10 cloves

1. Wash and peel the pears. Immediately put them in a bowl of water, with a splash of vinegar added, to prevent them turning brown.

2. Put the vinegar, sugar, lemon zest, cinnamon, and cloves in a saucepan, bring to a boil, and add the pears. Simmer over low heat for 2 hours.

3. Remove the pears from the syrup and put them into prepared jars. Strain the syrup through a sieve and pour it over the pears. Close the jars tightly. Turn the jars upside down, and leave them to cool on their lids.

Sweet-and-sour cherries are also delicious. I stone 2 pounds of washed Morello cherries, sprinkle them with 1 cup of sugar, and put them in the refrigerator to macerate for 2 days. I then pour 2 cups cold, good quality vinegar over the cherries and refrigerate for a further two days. I drain off the liquid, bring it to a boil, and pour it over the cherries. Refrigerate for a further two days. Put the cherries and juice in a saucepan and bring to a boil. Remove the cherries and gently simmer the juice for 15 minutes, then pour the hot juice over the cherries. Transfer to prepared jars, and close tightly.

Sweet-and-Sour Pumpkin
(Kürbis süß-sauer)

1 medium pumpkin
White wine vinegar
Sugar
5 cloves
1 cinnamon stick
Grated zest of 1 lemon

1. Cut the pumpkin into quarters, peel, and scoop out the seeds.

2. Cut the pumpkin flesh into medium-size chunks. Put them in a bowl and add enough vinegar to cover them. Allow to marinate for 12 hours.

3. Drain off the vinegar into a saucepan, reserving the pumpkin. To the vinegar add sugar to taste, the cloves, cinnamon, and lemon zest, and bring to a boil. (You need 3–4 cups of sugar for every 4 cups of wine vinegar). Skim the liquid, add the pumpkin, and simmer until tender.

4. Remove the pumpkin from the liquid with a slotted spoon and put it into prepared jars. Boil the liquid until very reduced and thick, then pour it over the pumpkin. Close the jars tightly, then store them upside down, on their lids, to cool.

Plums in Red Wine
(Zwetschgen in Rotwein)

5 pounds blue plums, stoned
4 cups sugar
2 cups good quality red wine
1 cup red wine vinegar
1 cinnamon stick
½ cup 80 or 100 proof vodka

1. Layer the plums in a very large jar, or a stone crock.

2. Put the sugar in a saucepan with the red wine and vinegar, and bring to a boil. Pour the hot syrup over the plums. Repeat this process daily, for two days.

3. On the fourth day, put the plums, syrup, and cinnamon stick in a saucepan and bring to a boil, then transfer back to the jar, or crock. Pour the alcohol over the plums and close the jar tightly.

Plums in red wine are a tasty accompaniment to game dishes and other dark meats.

Cranberries in Tokay
(Preiselbeeren in Tokajer)

2 pounds fresh cranberries
2 cups superfine granulated sugar
3–4 cloves
½ cup sweet Tokay wine

1. Pick over the berries very carefully, wash them, put them in a saucepan, and bring them to a boil over a medium heat stirring all the time. When they have boiled up once, skim off the resulting foam.

2. Add the sugar and cloves, and simmer, stirring all the time, until the sugar is completely dissolved.

3. Add the wine and simmer for a further 10 minutes.

4. Take the pan off the heat and allow the cranberries to cool a little, stirring all the time. Pour the cranberries into prepared jars. Close them tightly, stand them upside down on their lids, and allow them to cool.

Cranberry preserves is also delicious. Carefully sort 10 pounds of berries, wash them, and put them in a preserving pan. Bring to a boil over a medium heat, stirring all the time. After the fruit has boiled up, skim off the resulting foam. Add the sugar and simmer for 1 hour, until the preserves have thickened. Pour the preserves into jars, close tightly, and stand upside down, on the lids, and allow to cool.

Walnut Triangles
(Walnußecken)

5 tablespoons whole walnuts
2 teaspoons butter
14 ounces marzipan, or almond paste
6½ tablespoons confectioners' sugar
3 tablespoons raspberry eau-de-vie or schnapps
¼ pound good quality milk chocolate
½ cup halved walnuts, for decorating

1. Chop the whole walnuts. Melt the butter in a skillet and sauté the walnuts until golden.

2. Knead together the marzipan, or almond paste, the confectioners' sugar, chopped walnuts, and raspberry schnapps. Cover and refrigerate overnight.

3. Roll out the marzipan to ¼-inch thick. Cut out circles about 4 inches in diameter, then divide each circle into 6 triangles.

4. Break the chocolate into pieces and put in a bowl over a saucepan of barely simmering water. When the chocolate has melted, use it to coat the marzipan triangles. Press a halved walnut into the top of each and set on a wire rack to dry.

Ginger Nibbles taste equally delicous. Cut 4 pieces of preserved ginger into strips and dredge them with confectioners' sugar, or coat them in melted chocolate and leave them to dry on a wire rack.
In the past, walnut triangles, ginger nibbles, and homemade noodles, attractively packaged in linen bags, were a welcome gift to grandparents and aunts from our growing sons.

Apple Preserves
(Apfelkonfitüre)

2 pounds dessert apples
2 pounds sugar
Grated zest of 1 lemon
4 tablespoons brandy or Calvados

1. Wash, peel, and roughly chop the apples. Put them in a saucepan with just enough water to cover, bring to a boil, and simmer over medium heat until soft.

2. Purée the stewed apples through a sieve into a clean saucepan. Add the sugar and lemon zest, and bring to a boil. Simmer the purée until it is very thick, and you can see the base of the pan when you draw a wooden spoon through the purée.

3. Fold in the brandy or Calvados. Transfer the hot apple purée to prepared jars, or a stone crock. Seal the jars with a circle of baking parchment soaked in the alcohol.

In the past, nearly every back garden had its own apple tree. Somehow, commercially grown apples don't have the same depth of flavor. The recipe for this wonderful preserve originates from the turn of the nineteenth century, when it was often used to fill pancakes and in other sweet dishes.

Orange Marmalade
(Orangenmarmelade)

12 thin-skinned oranges
5 cups water
3 cloves
7 cups sugar
2 teaspoons citric acid
1 ⅔ cups brandy

1. Peel the oranges and remove all the pith. Divide into segments, remove the pits, reserving them, and chop the segments. Put the oranges in a saucepan, add enough water to cover, bring to a boil, and simmer for 30 minutes. Put the orange pits and cloves in a cheesecloth bag, add them to the oranges, and leave to infuse for 24 hours.

2. Bring the oranges to a boil with the sugar, and simmer for 3–4 hours, stirring occasionally. Add the citric acid. As soon as the marmalade starts to set, stir in the brandy. Remove the cheesecloth bag and pour the marmalade into prepared jars, close tightly, and store upside down to cool.

Sloe Juice
(Schlehensaft)

8 cups sloes
4 cups boiling water
13 tablespoons sugar (to every 4 cups juice)

1. Wash the sloes carefully, put them in a saucepan, and pour over the boiling water. There should be enough water to cover the fruit completely. Macerate in a warm place for 24 hours.

2. Strain through a sieve into a bowl. Put the liquid in a saucepan and bring to a boil. Pour it over the drained fruit. Allow the fruit to macerate for another 24 hours, then repeat this process.

3. Strain the fruit through a sieve, reserving the juice. Mix the juice and sugar in a saucepan, bring to a boil, and simmer gently for 40–50 minutes.

4. Pour the hot juice into prepared bottles and close tightly.

Collecting sloes is a laborious and prickly business, but it is worth it, because the juice tastes wonderful and is very, very good for you. The berries have the best flavor if they are harvested after the first frost.

Cherry Juice
(Roher Weichselsaft)

12 cups freshly pressed, filtered morello cherry juice (12 pounds of cherries)
8 cups boiled water
2 ounces argol
3 cups confectioners' sugar

1. Wash, remove the stalks, and pit the fruit, then press them to extract the juice. Line a sieve with cheesecloth and strain the juice through it.

2. Combine the juice, boiled water, and tartaric acid, and allow the mixture to stand for 24 hours.

3. Strain the juice through a cheesecloth-lined sieve and combine it with the confectioners' sugar.

4. Pour the juice into prepared bottles, close tightly, and store in a cool place.

Boiled morello cherry juice is also very flavorsome. Put 12 pounds of cherries in a saucepan, bruise them, add ½ cup wine, and bring to a boil stirring all the time. Strain through a sieve, add 7 cups confectioners' sugar for every 4 cups of juice, bring to a boil, and simmer until the juice coats the back of a spoon. Pour into prepared jars, close tightly, and store in a cool place. Try pouring the jelly-like cherry juice over vanilla ice cream for a dreamy dessert.

Elderberry Liqueur
(Holunderlikör)

4 pounds elderberries
6 cups sugar
1 vanilla pod, split
3 cups 100 proof vodka

1. Wash the berries. Put them in a saucepan with enough water to cover, and bring to a boil.

2. Line a sieve with cheesecloth, strain the fruit over a bowl, reserving the juice. Take care not to crush the berries and discard them.

3. Transfer the juice to a saucepan with the sugar and vanilla pod, bring to a boil, then simmer for 30 minutes.

4. Remove the vanilla pod and add the vodka. Pour the juice into prepared bottles and close tightly.

All kinds of berry liqueurs can be prepared in the same way. Liqueur made with red currants or black currants also tastes very good.

Advocaat
(Eierlikör)

1 cup sugar
2 cups water
12 fresh eggs
3 tablespoons fructose
3 tablespoons rum
1 cup low proof vodka

1. Put the sugar and water in a saucepan, bring to a boil, and simmer to form a sugar syrup, then allow to cool.

2. Beat the eggs with a hand-held electric mixer. Add the sugar syrup, at first drop by drop, beating all the time, then in a slow, steady stream.

3. Beat in the fructose and rum, then finally fold in the vodka.

4. Pour the advocaat into prepared bottles and cork tightly.

Rumtopf
(Rumtopf)

Seasonal fruits, starting with strawberries
then adding raspberries, morello cherries, apricots, peaches
blue plums, yellow plums, pears, and pineapple
Sugar equal to half the weight of the fruit
2 bottles 56% proof rum

1. Wash and hull the strawberries. Spread them out on a cloth to dry. Put them in a large stone crock, add half their weight in sugar, and enough rum to cover the strawberries by about one inch. In order to prevent the strawberries from floating to the top, put a saucer on top, and weigh it down. Seal the crock as tightly as possible, then allow it to rest in a cool cellar or the refrigerator. Shake the crock occasionally to help the sugar dissolve and prevent it settling on the base.

2. Check the level of liquid every 10 days and add more rum if necessary. There should always be one inch of rum above the fruits.

3. Layer the raspberries, unpitted cherries, and apricots in the same way. Apricots and peaches should be blanched briefly in boiling water and skinned. The apricots should be halved, the peaches quartered.

4. Blue and yellow plums should be stoned and halved. Use small pears if possible. Put them in boiling water, bring quickly to a boil, then remove and drain them on paper towels. Peel them and add them to the *rumtopf.*

5. Finish off the *rumtopf* with fresh pineapple. Peel it, cut it in half, remove the tough core, and chop the flesh into small chunks. Add to the rumtopf with half its weight in sugar.

6. Seal the crock tightly and store it in a cool place. Four weeks after the last batch of fruit was added, add a further ½ bottle of rum. Then allow the fruit to macerate until early December, preferably Christmas.

To me, rumtopf is a very special preserve – it provides a wonderful snapshot of the seasons. There is nothing nicer than enjoying the fruit you have picked throughout the year, at Christmas, in this most delicious way.